COLL

Cycling

in

SOMERSET
& WILTSHIRE

HarperCollins*Publishers*

Published by Collins
An imprint of HarperCollins*Publishers*
77–85 Fulham Palace Road
London W6 8JB

www.**fire**and**water**.com
www.bartholomewmaps.com

First published 2000
Copyright © HarperCollins*Publishers* Ltd 2000
Maps © Bartholomew Ltd 2000

Collins® is a registered trade mark of
HarperCollins*Publishers* Limited

Routes compiled by Neil Wheadon.
Design by Creative Matters Design Consultancy, Glasgow.
Typeset by Bob Vickers.

Photographs reproduced by kind permission of the following:
Britain on View/Stockwave pages 18, 40, 49, 56, 98, 101;
International Photobank pages 28, 36, 69; Andy Williams pages 5,
8, 11, 21, 24, 45, 63, 76, 77, 81.

The landscape is changing all the time. While every care has
been taken in the preparation of this guide, the Publisher accepts
no responsibility whatsoever for any loss, damage, injury or
inconvenience sustained or caused as a result of using this guide.

Printed in Italy

ISBN 0 00 448941 1
00/1/13

CONTENTS

Page

KEY TO ROUTES   4

LOCATION MAP AND KEY TO ROUTE MAPS   6

INTRODUCTION   How to use this guide   7

                      Cycling in Somerset & Wiltshire 7

                      Geology, geography and history   8

                      Preparing for a cycling trip   9

                      Cycling on-road   10

                      Cycling off-road   12

                      Local Tourist Information Centres 13

                      Local cycle hire   13

                      Local cycle shops   13

THE ROUTES   14–111

THE CTC   112

KEY TO ROUTES

Route		Grade	Distance km (miles)	Time to allow	Page
1	The Somerset Levels – Langport and Muchelney	easy	16.5 (10.5)	2–3 hours	14
2	Bradford-on-Avon and Rode	moderate	17.5 (11)	2–4 hours	17
3	The Nadder Valley – Tisbury and Teffont Magna	moderate	19 (12)	2–5 hours	20
4	Maiden Bradley, Shearwater and Longleat	moderate	21 (13)	2–4 hours	23
5	Ilminster, Winsham and the South Somerset Cycleway	moderate	24 (15)	2–3 hours	26
6	Martock and Montecute	moderate	24 (15)	2–4 hours	29
7	North Somerset Coast – Watchet and Cleeve Abbey	moderate	26.5 (16.5)	2–5 hours	32
8	The Quantock Hills	moderate	28 (17.5)	2–4 hours	35
9	Melksham, Corsham and Lacock	easy	29.5 (18.5)	2–3 hours	38
10	Street, Glastonbury and Wells	easy	32 (20)	2–4 hours	41
11	Bath, Lansdown and Bitton	strenuous	33 (20.5)	3–5 hours	44
12	Chiseldon, Avebury and Marlborough	moderate	43 (27)	3–6 hours	48
13	Swindon and the Cotswold Water Park	easy	48 (30)	3–5 hours	52
14	Malmesbury and Castle Combe	easy	49 (30.5)	3–5 hours	55
15	Ashton Court and Clevedon	moderate	51.5 (32)	3–6 hours	60
16	Marlborough and the Kennet and Avon Canal	easy	52.5 (32.5)	3–6 hours	64
17	Ilchester to Castle Cary	moderate	52 (32.5)	4–6 hours	68
18	Taunton and Bridgwater	easy	57 (35.5)	4–8 hours	72
19	Exmoor – Dunster to Porlock	strenuous	70.5 (44)	5–9 hours	77
20	The Polden Hills – Somerton to Glastonbury	moderate	74.5 (46.5)	5–9 hours	82
21	Salisbury and Shaftesbury	moderate	78 (48.5)	6–9 hours	86
22	Westbury and Salisbury Plain	moderate	78.5 (49)	6–10 hours	91
23	Frome to Wincanton	moderate	82 (51)	5–8 hours	96
24	Salisbury Plain and the Wylye Valley	moderate	87 (54)	5–9 hours	100
25	The grande randonnée	moderate	141 (88)	1–2 days	106

Distances have been rounded up or down to the nearest 0.5km (mile).

Route colour coding

	undemanding rides compiled specifically with families in mind 15–25km (10–15 miles)
	middle distance rides suitable for all cyclists 25–40km (15–25 miles)
	half-day rides for the more experienced and adventurous cyclist 40–60km (25–40 miles)
	challenging full-day rides over 60km (over 40 miles)
	grande randonnée – a grand cycling tour 100km (60 miles)

 Routes marked with this symbol are off-road or have off-road sections
(includes well-surfaced cycleways as well as rougher off-road tracks)

Wells Cathedral

LOCATION MAP

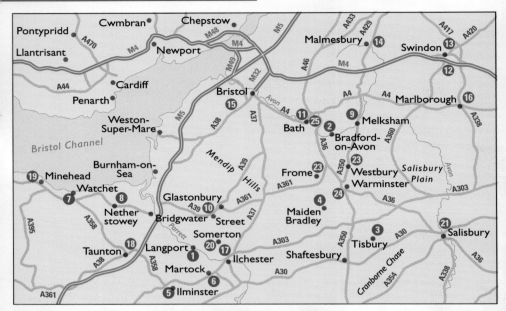

KEY TO ROUTE MAPS

M23 / Service area / A259	Motorway	
A259	'A' road / Dual carriageway	
B2130	'B' road / Dual carriageway	
	Good minor road	
	Minor road	
	Track / bridleway	
	Railway / station	
	Canal / river / lake	
	Ferry route	
50	Contour (height in metres)	

	Cycle route / optional route
	Start of cycle route
12	Route direction
B	Place of interest
	Public house
	Café / refreshments
✗	Restaurant
	Convenience store
i	Tourist Information Centre
P	Parking

☏	Telephone
⊼	Picnic site
▲	Camping site
♁	Public toilets
†	Place of worship
	Viewpoint
⌐	Golf course
	Tumulus
	Urban area
	Woodland

Height above sea level

50	100	150	200	300	400	500	600	700	800	900 metres
165	330	490	655	985	1315	1645	1975	2305	2635	2965 feet

INTRODUCTION

How to use this guide

Collins' *Cycling in Somerset & Wiltshire* has been devised for those who want trips out on their bicycles along quiet roads and tracks, passing interesting places and convenient refreshment stops without having to devise their own routes. Each of the 25 routes in this book has been compiled and ridden by an experienced cyclist for cyclists of all abilities.

Cycling in Somerset & Wiltshire is easy to use. Routes range from undemanding rides compiled specifically with families in mind to challenging full-day rides; the type of route is easily identified by colour coding (see page 5). At the start of each route an information box summarises: total distance (in kilometres/miles – distances have been rounded up or down throughout to the nearest 0.5km/mile and are approximate only); grade (easy, moderate or strenuous based on distance and difficulty); terrain; an average time to allow for the route; directions to the start of the route by car and, if appropriate, by train.

Each route is fully mapped and has concise, easy-to-follow directions. Comprehensive information on places of interest and convenient refreshment stops along each route are also given. Accumulated mileages within each route description give an indication of progress, while the profile diagram is a graphic representation of gradients along the route. These should be used as a guide only.

The following abbreviations are used in the route directions:

LHF	left hand fork
RHF	right hand fork
SO	straight on
SP	signpost
TJ	T junction
TL	turn left
TR	turn right
XR	crossroads

Cycling in Somerset & Wiltshire

The rides in this book run through Somerset and Wiltshire, covering an area from Malmesbury in the north to Ilminster in the south, and from Minehead in the west to Marlborough in the east. The routes stay away from busy main roads as much as possible to allow cyclists to discover the peaceful back lanes, tracks and cycleways that cross this area, passing all manner of museums, castles, historic houses and other attractions. There are steep sections to be tackled in some of the routes. This, however, is compensated for by spectacular views.

Various off-road routes are followed, including sections of the Bristol & Bath Railway Path, the Avon and the Wiltshire Cycleways, and canal towpaths. Some of these are part of the National Cycle Network. Be aware that these routes are often designated as multi-use, for walkers and horse riders as well as cyclists. The National Cycle Network is being developed by the charity Sustrans and will link urban areas with the countryside. For information contact Sustrans at 35 King Street, Bristol, BS1 4DZ, telephone (0117) 926 8893, www.sustrans.org.uk. Tourist Information Centres can provide information on local cycleways and Salisbury District Council operates the *Cycling & Walking Hotline*, offering free information on all aspects of cycling in the area — telephone (01980) 623255. Note that you will need a permit from British Waterways in order to cycle along the canal towpaths (small charge for the Kennet & Avon Canal, free for the Bridgewater & Taunton Canal). Telephone British Waterways on (01923) 201120 for further details.

Geology, geography and history

This part of south western England encompasses varied landscapes: the chalk uplands of Salisbury Plain; the limestone and sandstone ridge of the Mendip Hills; the limestone and granite Quantock Hills; and the high moorland of Exmoor. Between the Mendips and the Quantocks lie the peaty and flat plains of the Somerset Levels, criss-crossed with paths by the Stone Age inhabitants and drained during the Middle Ages. There are valleys and rivers, such as the Avon, Wylye, Yeo and Parrett, and the man-made waterways of the Kennet & Avon Canal and the Bridgewater & Taunton Canal, as well as the north Somerset coast and its traditional holiday resorts.

Throughout the area myth, legend and history have become deeply intertwined, and archaeological evidence is often difficult to investigate. There are ancient earthworks on Salisbury Plain, prehistoric stones at Avebury and Iron Age remains at Glastonbury. The Romans developed the area, constructing the Fosse Way and leaving evidence of a sacred spa at Bath. Local Arthurian legend dates from the late 5th century. Later history left its mark more plainly: the Saxon and Norman place names; the many old churches, Bath Abbey and the cathedrals of

Salisbury Cathedral from Church Fields

Glastonbury, Wells and Salisbury; and the 18th-century popularity of Bath, when it became the most fashionable place in the country.

The 18th century also saw the construction and development of the canals, increasing trade with other parts of the country (and decreasing local industries such as mining). The Victorians popularised holiday resorts such as Minehead and developed the railways, the remains of which provide many of today's traffic-free paths. Today Bath is an important commercial and ecclesiastical centre, Somerset's economy relies on agriculture, manufacturing and light industry, and Wiltshire's economy is sustained by agriculture, electronics, computing and tele-communications. And, as in many other parts of the country, leisure and tourism are becoming increasingly important to the local economies.

Preparing for a cycling trip

Basic maintenance

A cycle ride is an immense pleasure, particularly on a warm sunny day. Nothing is better than coasting along a country lane gazing over the countryside. Unfortunately, not every cycling day is as perfect as this, and it is important to make sure that your bike is in good order and that you are taking the necessary clothing and supplies with you.

Before you go out on your bicycle check that everything is in order. Pump the tyres up if needed, and check that the brakes are working properly and that nothing is loose – the brakes are the only means of stopping quickly and safely. If there is a problem and you are not sure that you can fix it, take the bike to a cycle repair shop – they can often deal with small repairs very quickly.

When you go out cycling it is important to take either a puncture repair kit or a spare inner tube – it is often quicker to replace the inner tube in the event of a puncture, though it may be a good idea to practise first. You also need a pump, and with a slow puncture the pump may be enough to get you home. To remove the tyre you need a set of tyre levers. Other basic tools are an Allen key and a spanner. Some wheels on modern bikes can be removed by quick release levers built into the bike. Take a lock for your bike and if you have to leave it at any time, leave it in public view and locked through the frame and front wheel to something secure.

What to wear and take with you

It is not necessary to buy specialised cycling clothes. If it is not warm enough to wear shorts wear trousers which are easy to move in but fairly close to the leg below the knee – leggings are ideal – as this stops the trousers catching the chain. If you haven't got narrow-legged trousers, bicycle clips will hold them in. Jeans are not a good idea as they are rather tight and difficult to cycle in, and if they get wet they take a long time to dry. If your shorts or trousers are thin you might get a bit sore from being too long on the saddle. This problem can be reduced by using a gel saddle, and by wearing thicker, or extra, pants. Once you are a committed cyclist you can buy cycling shorts; or undershorts which have a protective pad built in and which can be worn under anything. It is a good idea to wear several thin layers of clothes so that you can add or remove layers as necessary. A zip-fronted top gives easy temperature control. Make sure you have something warm and something waterproof.

If you wear shoes with a firm, flat sole you will be able to exert pressure on the pedals easily, and will have less work to do to make the bicycle move. Gloves not only keep your hands warm but protect them in the event that you come off, and cycling mittens which cushion your hands are not expensive. A helmet is not a legal requirement, but it will protect your head if you fall.

In general it is a good idea to wear bright clothing so that you can be easily seen by motorists, and this is particularly important when it is overcast or getting dark. If you might be out in the dark or twilight fit your bicycle with lights – by law your bicycle must have a reflector. You can also buy reflective bands for your ankles, or to wear over your shoulder and back, and these help motorists to see you.

You may be surprised how quickly you use up energy when cycling, and it is important to eat a carbohydrate meal before you set out. When planning a long ride, eat well the night before. You should eat small amounts of food regularly while you are cycling, or you may find that your energy suddenly disappears, particularly if there are hills or if the weather is cold. It is important to always carry something to eat with you – chocolate, bananas, biscuits – so that if you do start fading away you can restore yourself quickly. In warm weather you will sweat and use up fluid, and you always need to carry something to drink – water will do! Many bicycles have a fitment in which to put a water bottle, and if you don't have one a cycle shop should be able to fit one.

It is also a good idea to carry a small first aid kit. This should include elastoplasts or bandages, sunburn cream, and an anti-histamine in case you are stung by a passing insect.

It is a good idea to have a pannier to carry all these items. Some fit on the handlebars, some to the back of the seat and some onto a back rack. For a day's ride you probably won't need a lot of carrying capacity, but it is better to carry items in a pannier rather than in a rucksack on your back. Pack items that you are carrying carefully – loose items can be dangerous.

Getting to the start of the ride
If you are lucky you will be able to cycle to the start of the ride, but often transport is necessary. If you travel there by train, some sprinter services carry two bicycles without prior booking. Other services carry bicycles free in off-peak periods, but check the details with your local station. Alternatively, you could use your car – it may be possible to get a bike in the back of a hatchback if you take out the front wheel. There are inexpensive, easily fitted car racks which carry bicycles safely. Your local cycle store will be able to supply one to suit you.

Cycling on-road

Cycling on back roads is a delight with quiet lanes, interesting villages, good views and a smooth easy surface to coast along on. The cycle rides in this book are mainly on quiet roads but you sometimes cross busy roads or have stretches on B roads, and whatever sort of road you are on it is essential to ride safely. Always be aware of the possibility or existence of other traffic. Glance behind regularly, signal before you turn or change lane, and keep to the left. If there are motorists around, make sure that they have seen you before you cross their path. Cycling can be dangerous if you are competing for space with motor vehicles, many of which seem to have difficulty in seeing cyclists. When drivers are coming out of side roads, catch their eye before you ride in front of them.

You will find that many roads have potholes and uneven edges. They are much more difficult to

Farleigh Castle

spot when you are in a group because of the restricted view ahead, and therefore warnings need to be given. It is a good idea to cycle about a metre out into the road, conditions permitting, so that you avoid the worst of the uneven surfaces and to give you room to move in to the left if you are closely overtaken by a motor vehicle.

Other things to be careful of are slippery roads, particularly where there is mud or fallen leaves. Sudden rain after a period of dry weather often makes the roads extremely slippery. Dogs, too, are a hazard because they often move unpredictably, and sometimes like to chase cyclists. If you are not happy, stop or go slowly until the problem has passed.

Pedalling
Many modern bikes have 18 or 21 gears with three rings at the front and six or seven on the back wheel, and for much of the time you will find that the middle gear at the front with the range of gears at the back will be fine. Use your gears to find one that is easy to pedal along in so that your feet move round easily and you do not put too much pressure on your knees. If you are new to the bike and the gears it is a good idea to practise changing the gears on a stretch of flat, quiet road so that when you need to change gears quickly you will be ready to do so.

Cycling in a group
When cycling in a group it is essential to do so in a disciplined manner for your own, and others', safety. Do not ride too close to the bicycle in front of you – keep about a bicycle's length between you so that you will have space to brake or stop. Always keep both hands on the handlebars, except when signalling, etc. It is alright to cycle two abreast on quiet roads,

but if it is necessary to change from cycling two abreast to single file this is usually done by the outside rider falling in behind the nearside rider; always cycle in single file where there are double white lines, on busy roads, or on narrow and winding roads where you have a restricted view of the road ahead. Overtake on the right (outside) only; do not overtake on the inside.

It is important to pass information to other members of the group, for example:

car up – a vehicle is coming up behind the group and will be overtaking;

car down – a vehicle is coming towards the group;

single up – get into single file;

stopping – stopping, or

slowing/easy – slowing due to junction, etc., ahead;

on the left – there is an obstacle on the left, e.g. pedestrian, parked car;

pothole – pothole (and point towards it).

Accidents

In case of an accident, stay calm and, if needed, ring the emergency services on 999. It is a good idea to carry a basic first aid kit and perhaps also one of the commercial foil wraps to put around anyone who has an accident to keep them warm. If someone comes off their bicycle move them and the bike off the road if it is safe to do so. Get someone in the party to warn approaching traffic to slow down, and if necessary ring for an ambulance.

Cycling off-road

All the routes in this book take you along legal rights of way – bridleways, byways open to all traffic and roads used as public paths – it is illegal to cycle along footpaths. Generally the off-road sections of the routes will be easy if the weather and ground are dry. If the weather has been wet and the ground is muddy, it is not a good idea to cycle along bridleways unless you do not mind getting dirty and unless you have a mountain bike which will not get blocked up with mud. In dry weather any bicycle will be able to cover the bridleway sections, but you may need to dismount if the path is very uneven.

Off-road cycling is different to cycling on the road. The average speed is lower, you will use more energy, your riding style will be different and there is a different set of rules to obey – the off-road code:

1 Give way to horse riders and pedestrians, and use a bell or call out to warn someone of your presence.

2 Take your rubbish with you.

3 Do not light fires.

4 Close gates behind you.

5 Do not interfere with wildlife, plants or trees.

6 Use only tracks where you have a right of way, or where the landowner has given you permission to ride.

7 Avoid back wheel skids, which can start erosion gulleys and ruin the bridleway.

Some of the off-road rides take you some miles from shelter and civilisation – take waterproofs, plenty of food and drink and basic tools – especially spare inner tubes and tyre repair equipment. Tell someone where you are going and approximately when you are due back. You are more likely to tumble off your bike riding off-road, so you should consider wearing a helmet and mittens with padded palms.

Local Tourist Information Centres

Somerset

Bath
Abbey Churchyard, Bath
Telephone (01225) 477101

Bridgwater
50 High Street, Bridgwater
Telephone (01278) 427652

Somerset Visitor Centre
Sedgemoor Services, M5 South, Axbridge
Telephone (01934) 750833

Cheddar
The Gorge, Cheddar
Telephone (01934) 744071

Frome
2 Bridge Street, Frome
Telephone (01373) 467271

Glastonbury
9 High Street, Glastonbury
Telephone (01458) 832954

Minehead
17 Friday Street, Minehead
Telephone (01643) 702624

Taunton
Paul Street, Taunton
Telephone (01823) 336344

Wells
Market Place, Wells
Telephone (01749) 672552

Exmoor Visitor Centres

Dulverton
Telephone (01398) 323841

Dunster
Telephone (01643) 821835

Bruton
Telephone (01749) 812851

Castle Cary
Telephone (01963) 351628

Clarks Village, Street
Telephone (01458) 447384

Ilminster
Telephone (01460) 57294

Langport
Telephone (01458) 253527

Porlock
Telephone (01643) 863150

Quantock Information Centre
Telephone (01278) 733642

Somerton
Telephone (01458) 274070

Watchet
Telephone (01984) 634565

Wiltshire

Amesbury
Flower Lane, Amesbury
Telephone (01980) 622833

Avebury
The Great Barn, Avebury
Telephone (01672) 539425

Bradford-on-Avon
34 Silver Street, Bradford-on-Avon
Telephone (01225) 865797

Corsham
31 High Street, Corsham
Telephone (01249) 714660

Devizes
39 St Johns Street, Devizes
Telephone (01380) 729408

Malmesbury
Market Lane, Malmesbury
Telephone (01666) 823748

Marlborough
25 George Lane Car Park, Marlborough
Telephone (01672) 513989

Salisbury
Fish Row, Salisbury
Telephone (01722) 334956

Shaftesbury
8 Bell Street, Shaftesbury
Telephone (01747) 853514

Swindon
37 Regent Street, Swindon
Telephone (01793) 530328

Warminster
Central Car Park, Warminster
Telephone (01985) 218548

Local cycle hire

Batchelors Cycles
72 Market Place, Warminster
Telephone (01985) 213221

Bicycle Chain
St James Street, Taunton
Telephone (01823) 252499

Bike City
31 Broad Street, Wells
Telephone (01749) 671711

Bow Bridge Cycles
Langport & River Parrett Visitor Centre, Langport
Telephone (01458) 250350

Hayballs Cycles
26–30 Winchester Street, Salisbury
Telephone (01722) 411378

Lock Inn
Bradford-on-Avon
Telephone (01225) 868068

Pedlars
8 Magdalene Street, Glastonbury
Telephone (01458) 831117

Local cycle shops

Batchelors Cycles, Bicycle Chain (Taunton), Bike City, Hayballs Cycles, Pedlars (see above).

Bicycle Chain
101a Taunton Road, Bridgwater
Telephone (01278) 423640

Street Cycle Company
157 High Street, Street
Telephone (01458) 447882

THE SOMERSET LEVELS – LANGPORT AND MUCHELNEY

Route information

 Distance 16.5km (10.5 miles)

 Grade Easy

Terrain Flat throughout, except for one short but steep hill. The optional off-road section follows a well-surfaced railway path.

 Time to allow 2–3 hours.

Getting there by car Langport is north of Ilchester, via the A303 and A372. There are two free car parks in town. The route starts from the Whatley car park (incorporates Cocklemoor long-stay car park). The entrance is opposite the clock on the High Street.

 Getting there by train Although the railway passes through Langport, there is no station in the town.

A route around the Somerset Levels. Starting from Langport the route heads west towards pancake flat West Sedge Moor. Turning south, a short steep climb up to Red Hill provides opportunities to walk to fabulous viewpoints. On through Curry River and Drayton to Muchelney. There is a choice for the return to Langport – either on-road taking in the old town of Langport, or via the Parrett Cycleway.

Route description

From Whatley car park, exit to the High Street to TL at TJ, SP Taunton A378. Cross River Parrett and leave Langport.

1 TR, SP Wick/Burrowbridge. Pass SP weak bridge. Continue on this road.

2 TL, SP Oath/Heale/Curry Rivel (4.5km/ 3 miles). Cross large bridge. After 1.5km (1 mile) ascend a 20% hill. Just after passing Red Hill on LHS:

3 TR, no SP. Pass Hillcrest Cottage then footpath to Burton Pynsent Monument on RHS.

4 TL at TJ, SP Curry Rivel/Langport. Immediately TR, no SP (8km/5 miles), for descent, passing Westfield on RHS.

5 TL at TJ, no SP. Continue along this flat narrow lane.

6 TL at TJ, no SP. Then TR, no SP (but just before Curry Rivel village SP). Pass Corner Cottage on LHS.

7 TR at XR, SP Drayton/Muchelney. Continue through Drayton following SP Muchelney, passing Drayton Arms pub on RHS. Pass cycle SP and:

8 For off-road option TL, SP Parrett Cycleway. Pass through two gates and continue along gravelled cycleway for 1.5km (1 mile). TR at XR, SP Huish Drove, and immediately TL, SP Parrett Cycleway. Continue and pass Langport and River Parrett Visitor Centre on RHS. Arrive A378 and TR, no SP.

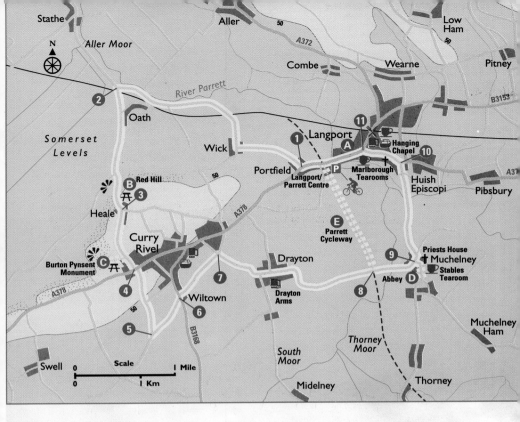

Cross River Parrett and continue into Langport to complete the route.

To stay on-road, continue SO towards Muchelney.

9 To visit Muchelney Abbey, TR at TJ for 200m, bearing right to entrance. Otherwise, TL at TJ, SP Langport (Priests House opposite) and continue towards Langport.

10 TL at TJ, no SP (opposite post box, following stone wall on RHS). Continue under Hanging Chapel and pass church on LHS.

11 TL at TJ (effectively SO), SP Taunton. Continue into Langport to finish the ride.

16.5km (10.5 miles)

Places of interest along the route

Ⓐ Langport

Situated on the River Parrett, Langport has been a trading centre since Saxon times. The original settlement was on Langport Hill, the site of the Hanging Chapel. Standing on an arch over the road, the chapel was originally used for worship but has since housed a school, militia arms store and a museum, and it is now a Free Masons' lodge. The **Langport and River Parrett Visitor Centre** describes life on the Somerset Levels and Moors, and contains a Discovery Room where visitors can explore the River Parrett trail from source to mouth. Cycle hire shop and outdoor store on site. Open April to September, daily 1000–1800; October to March, Tuesday–Sunday 1000–1600. Admission free. Telephone (01458) 250350.

Ⓑ Red Hill

Managed by the National Trust, Red Hill provides an great picnic site with panoramic views across West Sedge Moor. Free access at all times.

Ⓒ Burton Pynsent Monument, Stoneleigh

To the left of Stoneleigh's iron gates is a footpath leading to the imposing monument which commands a glorious view over West Sedge Moor. Although the monument entrance is sealed, the 17th- and 18th-century graffiti carved into the base provides an intriguing insight into the past. Free access at all reasonable times.

Ⓓ Muchelney

South of Langport is the medieval monastic settlement of Muchelney. **Muchelney Abbey** was founded in the 10th century on the site of an earlier abbey. It is now mostly ruined except for

Food and drink

Plenty of choice in Langport. There is a convenience store and pub in Curry Rivel.

☕ **Marlborough Tearooms, Langport**
At the River Parrett end of the High Street, serving cream teas.

🍴 **Drayton Arms, Drayton**
Meals available. Also, camping and caravan park.

✖ **Stables Tearoom, Muchelney**
Typical tearoom fare in a converted stable complete with hay nets. Open summer only.

the remarkably complete 15th-century Bishops House. English Heritage property. Gift shop selling snacks, cold drinks and ice creams. Open daily, April to September 1000–1800; October, 1000–dusk. Charge. Telephone (01458) 250644. Adjacent to the abbey is the **Parish Church of St Peter and St Paul**. Built by the abbots in the 15th century, the church features 12th-century stained glass and Tudor ceiling paintings. Open daily in summer. The priests serving the church lived in the **Priests House**. A privately occupied National Trust property, the house is open to the public April to September, Sunday and Monday 1400–1700. Charge. Telephone (01458) 252621.

Ⓔ Parrett Cycleway

The Parrett Cycleway follows the old Yeovil to Langport railway line for 2.5km (1.5 miles), from the visitor centre at Langport to the village of Muchelney.

BRADFORD-ON-AVON AND RODE

Route information

 Distance 17.5km (11 miles)

 Grade Moderate

 Terrain Mostly well-surfaced country lanes with one section of B road. There are several steep climbs (the first out of Bradford-on-Avon is the longest).

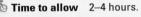

 Time to allow 2–4 hours.

 Getting there by car Bradford-on-Avon is south east of Bath on the A363. There are several long-term car parks in the town – the most convenient is by the station (pay and display but free on Sundays).

 Getting there by train There is a railway station at Bradford-on-Avon. Telephone (0345) 484950 for information.

From the lovely town of Bradford-on-Avon a steep climb takes you to the village of Westwood from where the route turns south. You will see Westbury White Horse in the distance, as a series of quiet, undulating lanes lead you past Westwood Manor, Farleigh Hungerford Castle and Rode Bird Garden (a good stop for lunch). Following a tour of the pretty village of Rode, the ride follows a B road back to Bradford (the road is straight and flat, offering good visibility and safety).

Places of interest along the route

A **Bradford-on-Avon**

Bradford-on-Avon, built mostly of Bath stone, is on the River Avon. In the centre of the town is a 17th-century arched bridge on top of which is a tiny lock up, formerly a chapel. Close to the bridge is the **Bradford-on-Avon Museum** (on first floor of library). The museum contains a reconstructed pharmacy that stood in the town for 120 years. Open Easter to October, Wednesday–Saturday 1030–1600, Sunday 1400–1600. Admission free. Telephone (01225) 863280. The Saxon **Church of St Lawrence** was rediscovered in 1856 and is believed to date from between the 7th and 10th centuries. Free access. To the south of town is **Barton Farm Country Park**. Bounded by the Kennet and Avon Canal and the River Avon, the park comprises 14.5ha (36 acres) of lovely countryside, perfect for a picnic. In the park, standing below the canal embankment, is the **Tithe Barn**. Built in the 14th century and originally used to store grain, the barn is now the second largest of it's kind in England. The related granary and cow byres now house craft shops and galleries. Tearoom. Free admission to park at all reasonable times. Telephone Bradford-on-Avon Tourist Information Centre for further information on (01225) 865797.

B **Westwood Manor, Westwood**

In 1518 the rich clothier Thomas Horton converted a minor house into Westwood Manor. Over the years it has been gradually remodelled and is today noted for the late Gothic and

Jacobean windows and the Great Hall. The garden features a modern topiary. National Trust property. Open April to September, Sunday, Tuesday and Wednesday 1400–1700. Charge. Telephone (01225) 863374.

Ⓒ Farleigh Hungerford Castle, Farleigh Hungerford

Set in the picturesque valley of the River Frome, Farleigh Hungerford Castle was originally built by Sir Thomas Hungerford in the 14th century. Despite the fact that the northern part of the castle was demolished during the 17th century, much of the original building remains, including the mid-14th-century parish church of St Leonard, with its medieval wall paintings and eight lead coffins. Stroll, relax or picnic in the grounds. Audio-tour and gift shop. English Heritage property. Open April to October, daily 1000–1800; November to March, Wednesday–Sunday 1000–1600. Charge. Telephone (01225) 754026.

Westbury White Horse

Ⓓ Rode Bird Garden, Rode

The garden features over 200 different species of tropical birds from around the world. The centre pioneered captive breeding – it was the first to breed Red Tailed Amazons and holds the stud book for Black Cockatoos. On-site attractions include a pet's corner, children's play area, 7ha (17 acres) of formal Victorian gardens and a narrow gauge steam railway. Café (open summer only). Open daily, summer 1000–1800; winter 1000–dusk (trains run daily throughout the summer and at spring and autumn half-term holidays). Charge. Telephone (01373) 830326.

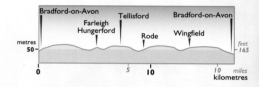

Route description

Leave the railway station car park to TR at roundabout along Frome Road, SP Frome. Cross mini roundabout (park on right). Immediately after crossing the canal:

1 TR, no SP, passing Canal Cottage Bridge House on LHS. Climb Jones Hill (initially steep).

2 TL at staggered XR, no SP (pass blue width limit SP on RHS). Continue for gentle descent with sweeping views (including Westbury White Horse straight ahead).

3 TL at TJ, SP Bradford/Trowbridge.

4 TR, SP Westwood Manor (opposite New Inn). Pass entrance to Westwood Manor on LHS. Continue along narrow lane with care – there is a steep descent at the end.

5 TR at TJ, no SP (5.5km/3.5 miles). Cross two small bridges for short, steep climb. Pass Farleigh Hungerford Castle on RHS.

6 TL, SP Tellisford/Rode, along narrow undulating lane.

7 TL at TJ, SP Rode (opposite Mill Restaurant). Cross bridge.

8 TR into Rode, no SP, to TL at TJ, no SP but opposite Cross Keys pub. Continue through village passing war memorial on RHS.

9 TR at XR, SP Bradford/Trowbridge (10km/6 miles). Pass two-spired church on LHS.

10 TL at XR, SP Wingfield/Bradford. Continue along this straight B road through Wingfield, passing the Poplars on LHS.

11 SO at XR (traffic lights) SP Bradford/Westwood. Continue on this road into Bradford-on-Avon to finish the ride.

17.5km (11 miles)

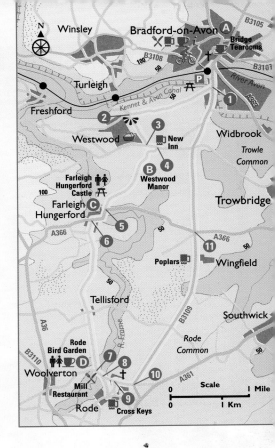

Food and drink

Plenty of choice in Bradford-on-Avon. There is a pub and convenience store at Westwood and a pub and restaurant in Rode. Refreshments are also available at Rode Bird Garden.

Bridge Tearooms, Bradford-on-Avon
Award-winning tearooms. The waitresses serve in Victorian dresses and the cakes are enormous.

The Poplars, Wingfield
Meals available.

THE NADDER VALLEY – TISBURY AND TEFFONT MAGNA

Route information

- **Distance**   19km (12 miles)

- **Grade**   Moderate

- **Terrain**   Quiet lanes and two short sections of B road. There are two short steep climbs.

- **Time to allow**   2–5 hours.

- **Getting there by car**   Tisbury is reached from the A30 Shaftesbury to Wilton road. There is a free car park on The Avenue.

- **Getting there by train**   There is a railway station at Tisbury. Telephone (0345) 484950 for travel information.

Starting from Tisbury the route heads east along the Nadder Valley, passing attractive lakes and buildings on the way. A short section of B road leads to a quiet minor road, past Dinton Park (a great place for a walk or picnic). On for a short steep climb to Teffont Magna, where a detour to the delightful Farmer Giles Farmstead is recommended. A final section of B road and a subsequent quiet lane leads back to Tisbury.

Places of interest along the route

(A) Tisbury

The town is situated on the convergence of the Rivers Nadder and Sem and is noted for its 14th- to 18th-century architecture. The largest existing Medieval Tithe Barn in Britain is at Place Farm. The partially restored ruins of **Old Wardour Castle** are 3km (2 miles) outside the town in an attractive location between the river and woodland. Originally built in the late 14th century, the castle was twice besieged in the Civil War, first by the parliamentarians and then by the royalist troops. English Heritage property. Open April to September, daily 1000–1800; October, daily 1000–1700; November to March, Wednesday–Sunday 1000–1300 and 1400–1600. Telephone (01747) 870487.

(B) Phillips House, Tisbury

Completed in 1812, Phillips House is a good example of a neo-Grecian house. The ground floor is open to the public and features a central staircase of Portland stone with a lantern window above. Surrounding the house are the recently restored and landscaped grounds of Dinton Park. National Trust property. House open April to October, Monday 1300–1700, Saturday 1000–1300. Park open throughout the year. Charge for admission to house only. Telephone (01985) 843600.

(C) Farmer Giles Farmstead

Farmer Giles Farmstead is a working dairy farm and provides a wonderful opportunity to appreciate the routine of a modern farm. Visitors can milk a cow or bottle feed a lamb. Also exhibitions on dairying and farming through the ages. For children there is the added bonus of an adventure playground, lots of tractors and a bouncy castle. Café and indoor picnic area. Open March to November, daily 1000–1800; December to February, weekends only. Charge. Telephone (01722) 716338.

Teffont Magna

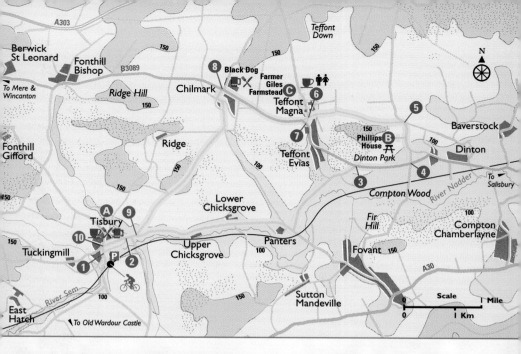

Route description

Leave the railway station to TR at TJ (effectively SO). Pass playing fields on RHS.

1 TR along The Avenue, SP Parking. Pass car park on RHS.

2 TR at TJ along Court Street, no SP. Leave Tisbury along this undulating country lane and continue on this road through Chicksgrove to descend, passing river on RHS.

3 TR at TJ, SP Salisbury.

4 TL at XR, SP Wylye (8km/5 miles). Pass Dinton Park and then Phillips House on LHS and climb steeply. At top of hill:

5 TL at XR, SP Teffont/Chilmark.

6 To visit Farmer Giles Farmstead, TR at TJ. Otherwise, to continue route TL at TJ, SP Salisbury.

7 TR at TJ, SP Mere/Wincanton. Continue on this road into Chilmark, passing Black Dog pub on RHS.

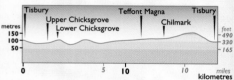

8 TL, SP Chilmark/Tisbury. Follow SP Tisbury and climb.

9 TR at TJ, SP Tisbury. **17.5km (11 miles)**

10 TL along Park Street, no SP. Then TL at TJ opposite garage, no SP. Descend through town and return to the station to finish the ride.

19km (12 miles)

Food and drink

There are several places to eat in Tisbury and refreshments are available at Farmer Giles Farmstead.

 Black Dog, Chilmark
Pub and restaurant.

MAIDEN BRADLEY, SHEARWATER AND LONGLEAT

Route information

Distance   21km (13 miles)

Grade   Moderate

Terrain   Two climbs and a glorious descent along tarmac roads.

Time to allow   2–4 hours.

Getting there by car   Maiden Bradley is on the B3092, 9.5km (6 miles) south of Frome. There is car parking in the village.

Getting there by train   There is no practical rail access to this route.

Starting from the church at Maiden Bradley, the route follows a quiet flat road to Barngate Game Reserve and the beautiful lake at Shearwater. A steady uphill climb through the woods of Longleat Estate is the prelude to a wonderful descent towards the house itself, passing the safari park's rhinos and lions. On through the gatehouse for a climb back to Maiden Bradley.

Places of interest along the route

Ⓐ Maiden Bradley

Maiden Bradley is a pretty village noted for its church and the white marble memorial to Sir Edward Seymour. Built by his grandson, the memorial is a catalogue of tributes to this former speaker of the House of Commons.

Ⓑ Barngate Game Reserve

To the east of the Longleat Estate, the focus of the reserve is Shearwater Lake, a magnet for anglers and sailors. Surrounding the lake are woods, criss-crossed by bridleways and paths on which you may see deer, badgers, foxes or even wild boar. Café, children's play area and ice cream sales by the lake. Reserve open all year.

Ⓒ Longleat

On of the finest example of Elizabethan architecture in Britain, Longleat House stands at the centre of the estate, well-known as a safari park. The estate was acquired in 1541 by Sir John Thynne who subsequently started construction of the house which was still unfinished on his death in 1580. The 6th Marquis of Bath started the safari park in an attempt to balance the books after World War II. Today the park contains many species of animals including giraffes, elephants, rhinos and of course the lions. Other attractions include the world's longest Hedge Maze, boat trips, Doctor Who Exhibition and an Adventure Castle. A safari bus service is available for cyclists from Pet's Corner (charge). The pleasant Cellar Tearooms are sited beneath the house (free admission). The estate is open mid March–October, daily: house 1000–1800; safari park 1000–1700; other attractions 1100–1730. Although bicycles may enter free of charge, there is a charge for most of the attractions. Telephone (01985) 844400.

Food and drink

There is a village store and pub at Maiden Bradley and a store at Horningsham. Refreshments are available at Shearwater Lake and Longleat.

Bath Arms, Crockerton
Bar meals and outside seating.

Bath Arms, Horningham
Ivy fronted pub offering accommodation and a restaurant.

Route description

Start from the large church (blue clockface) in Maiden Bradley. Head north along the B3092 towards Frome, passing Somerset Arms on RHS.

1 TR at XR along High Street, SP Salisbury/Warminster.

2 TL, SP Shearwater/Warminster/Shaftesbury. Gently descend to pass Barngate Game Reserve and Shearwater Lake on LHS. Enter Crockerton.

3 TL at TJ, SP Wiltshire Cycleway (Bath Arms on LHS of junction). Descend then climb.

Longleat House

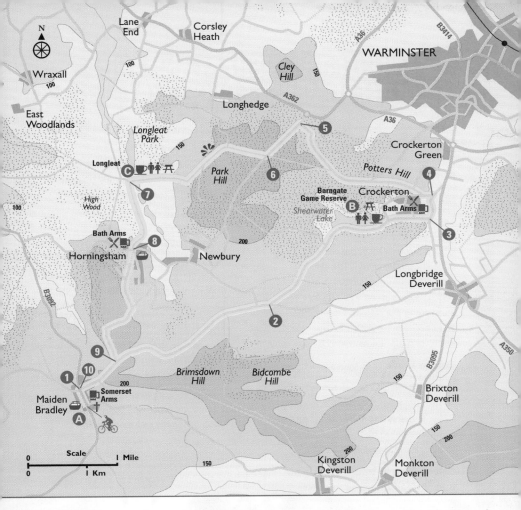

4 TL, SP Potters Hill (8km/5 miles). Keep climbing through woods, ignoring next TL to Potters Hill.

5 TL at TJ just before Picket Post round-about, no SP. Pass Centre Parks entrance on LHS. Just after forestry building on RHS:

6 TR, no SP. Pass multiple no parking bollards and continue through official entrance to Longleat (bicycles free). Descend towards the house with the safari park on RHS.

7 To visit the tearoom, TR and pass to right of house through gates. Otherwise, TL at XR in front of house, no SP. Gently climb to pass through gatehouse, for a stiffer climb ahead.

8 SO at XR, SP Maiden Bradley/Mere (16.5km/10.5 miles). Continue climbing.

9 TR at TJ, SP Maiden Bradley/Bruton.

10 TL at XR, SP Mere/Stourhead/Wincanton/Gillingham. Return to church to finish the ride. **21km (13 miles)**

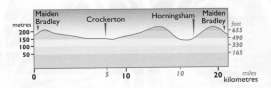

ILMINSTER, WINSHAM AND THE SOUTH SOMERSET CYCLEWAY

Route information

Distance 24km (15 miles)

Grade Moderate

Terrain Although on-road through-out, there are two short sections where the tarmac is patchy and care should be taken. The roads are especially undulating south of the A30 – these can be avoided by shortening the ride and going from direction 2 to direction 8, reducing the total distance to 16km (10 miles).

Time to allow 2–3 hours.

Getting there by car Ilminster is in south Somerset, signposted from the A303. There is a long-term car park (Shudrick Lane) by the Tourist Information Centre in town.

Getting there by train There is no practical rail access to this route.

Starting in Ilminster the route heads south, passing Cricket St Thomas Wildlife Park. On along more undulating roads through Winsham. The route then turns north along part of the South Somerset Cycleway (good views here). A short ride on the A30 leads to country lanes and the return to Ilminster.

Route description

Start by the Tourist Information Centre and leave Shudrick Lane car park to TL at TJ, no SP.

Cycle out of Ilminster and pass Moolham Lane on LHS.

1 TL, SP Cricket Malherbie/Windwistle/Dowlish Wake. Climb steadily passing pretty church on LHS (opposite Manor Farm).

2 To shorten the route (avoiding undulating roads) TL here along A30 and continue route by TL at direction 8. Otherwise, TR at TJ onto A30, no SP.   *6.5km (4 miles)*

3 TL, SP Cricket St Thomas. Follow SP to wildlife park. After visit, follow exit SP and climb.

4 TL at TJ, no SP.   *9km (5.5 miles)*

5 TL, no SP (9.5km/6 miles). Continue along this intermittently rough lane.

6 TR at TJ, no SP (11km/7 miles). Then TL sharply at XR onto Fore Street, no SP (convenience store opposite). Leave Winsham to climb gradually, admiring views to right.

7 TL at TJ onto A30, no SP.

8 TR, no SP (road SP Unsuitable for Motors). Descend grass centred track WITH CARE – it is steep at end.

9 SO at XR, no SP.

10 TL, SP Dowlish Wake.

11 TL to visit Perry's Cider Mills. Otherwise, TR at TJ, SP Kingstone/Ilminster/Crewkerne.

12 TR at TJ, SP Ilminster/Crewkerne. Then TL at TJ, no SP. Enter Ilminster.

13 TL at TJ, no SP.

14 TL, SP Tourist Information.

15 TL, SP Chard/Axminster and return to the Tourist Information Centre to complete the route.   *24km (15 miles)*

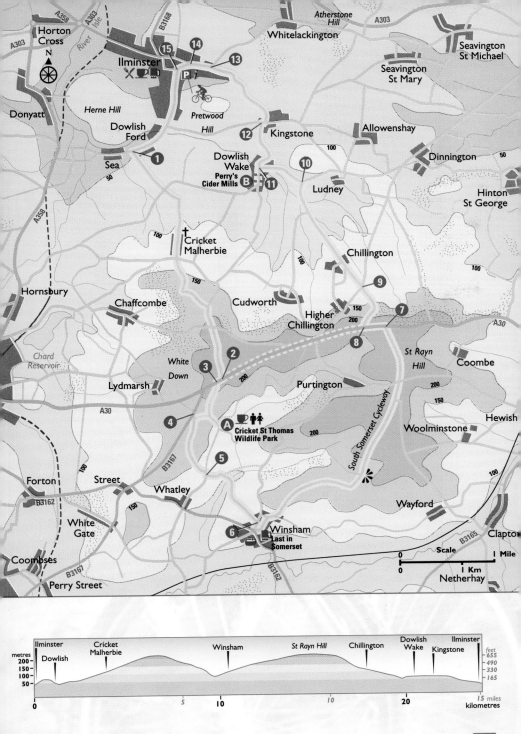

Horton Cross
A358
A303 Isle
B3168
Atherstone Hill
A303
Whitelackington
Seavington St Michael

Ilminster
N
River Isle
15 14
13
Seavington St Mary

Donyatt
Herne Hill
Pretwood Hill
Kingstone
12
Allowenshay
Dinnington
50

Dowlish Ford
Sea
1
Dowlish Wake
Perry's Cider Mills
B
11
10
Ludney
100
Hinton St George

100
Cricket Malherbie
Chillington
100

Hornsbury
150
Chaffcombe
Cudworth
Higher Chillington
9
St Rayn Hill
Coombe

Chard Reservoir
White Down
3 2
150
200
8
7
A30
Hewish

Lydmarsh
A30
Purtington
200
150
Woolminstone

4
Cricket St Thomas Wildlife Park
A
South Somerset Cycleway
200

Forton
Street
B3167
5
Whatley
Wayford
100
B3165
Clapton

White Gate
150
6
Winsham
Last in Somerset
Scale
0   1 Mile
0   1 Km
Netherhay

Coombses
B3162
B3167
Perry Street
B3162

metres
200
150
100
50

Ilminster
Dowlish
Cricket Malherbie
Winsham
St Rayn Hill
Chillington
Dowlish Wake
Kingstone
Ilminster

feet
655
490
330
165

0
5
10
10
20
15 miles
kilometres

Places of interest along the route

Cricket St Thomas Wildlife Park, Cricket St Thomas

Visitors have the opportunity to walk through a wood where three species of lemur roam freely. There is a miniature railway ride through several paddocks, allowing glimpses of the house made famous in the TV comedy *To the Manor Born*. Also falconry displays, pets' corner and children's playground. Coffee shop serving hot snacks, fast food and cakes. Gift shop. Open daily, summer 1000–1800; winter 1000–dusk. Charge. Telephone (01460) 30111.

Perry's Cider Mills, Dowlish Wake

The cider making equipment and presses are on display, together with photographs and a video illustrating cider making. Also a small museum on rural life. A range of farmhouse ciders may be sampled before purchase at the farm shop. Open all year, Monday–Friday 0900–1730, Saturday 0930–1630, Sunday 1000–1300, Bank Holidays 0930–1630. Admission free. Telephone (01460) 52681.

Food and drink

Plenty of choice in Ilminster. There is a small shop in Winsham and refreshments are available at the wildlife park.

Last in Somerset, Winsham
The pub is well-known for its speciality pies.

Somerset landscape

MARTOCK AND MONTECUTE

Route information

Distance   24km (15 miles)

Grade   Moderate

Terrain   On-road using mostly gently undulating lanes. There is one steep climb up to Ham Hill.

Time to allow   2–4 hours.

Getting there by car   Martock is west of Yeovil, signposted from the A303. There is free long-term parking 100m from the Market Place, the start of the route.

Getting there by train   There is no practical railway access to this ride.

From Martock the route heads west to the small town of South Petherton. Crossing the A303, you follow a quiet lane for a steep climb up Ham Hill. The reward is wonderful views and a delightful place to picnic, eat ice cream or relax in the pub. On for a steep descent into the historic village of Montecute and a visit to Tintinhull Garden, before the return to Martock. If you do not want to visit the gardens, or are a little short of time, the minor roads from Montecute to Stoke sub Hamden and from there to Martock are worth considering.

Places of interest along the route

(A) The Treasurers House, Martock

This is the second oldest inhabited house in Somerset and comprises a two-storey hall dating from 1293, and a 15th-century kitchen. The house has recently been refurbished by the National Trust. Open April to September, Sunday, Monday and Tuesday 1400–1700. Charge. Telephone (01935) 825801.

(B) Ham Hill Country Park

Rising to over 91.5m (300 feet), Ham Hill Country Park covers an area of 56.5ha (140 acres). Once an Iron Age fort, today the hummocky appearance is due to hundreds of years of quarrying. There are magnificent views over the surrounding countryside. The park has plenty of picnic areas, information boards and toilets, with the added advantage of a good pub serving food, the Prince of Wales. Free access at all reasonable times. Telephone the ranger for further information on (01935) 823617.

(C) Montecute TV and Radio Memorabilia Museum, Montecute

The museum contains a marvellous collection of over 400 radios and radiograms dating from 1920 through to 1970. There is also an extensive collection of toys, annuals, magazines and memorabilia from numerous radio and TV programmes. As if that is not enough, the Mad Hatters Tearoom and Garden serves home-made cakes and clotted cream teas. There is an outdoor play area for younger children. Open April to October, Monday–Saturday

1000–1700, Sunday 1100–1730 (closed Tuesday early and late season). Charge for museum only. Telephone (01935) 823024.

D Montecute House, Montecute

Built between 1588 and 1601 by Sir Edward Phelips, this magnificent Elizabethan house with an H-shaped ground plan portrays many Renaissance features including plasterwork, chimney pieces and heraldic glass, as well as portraits from the National Portrait Gallery. Outside there are 10ha (25 acres) of formal gardens and parkland. The house and grounds featured in the film *Sense and Sensibility*. Shop and tearoom. Open April to October, daily (except Tuesday afternoons) 1100–1730. Telephone (01935) 823289.

E Tintinhull Garden, Tintinhull

The small manor house garden at Tintinhull was designed by Phyllis Reiss and is divided by clipped yew hedges and walls into seven unique rooms, including a pool garden, fountain garden and a traditional kitchen garden. National Trust property. Tearoom. Open April to September, Wednesday–Sunday and Bank Holiday Mondays 1200–1800. Charge. Telephone (01935) 822545.

Route description

Start from the centre of Martock at the Market Place (easily recognised by the Market House which is supported on pillars). Head west towards church, passing Treasurers House on LHS.

1 TR along a flat lane, SP South Petherton/Parrett Works, passing SP South Somerset Cycleway. Climb a short hill to descend into South Petherton, bearing left at bottom of hill along Prigg Lane.

2 TL at TJ, no SP (TR for town/toilets). Pass converted church (David Hall Arts Centre) on LHS, TR along South Street and leave town.

3 TL at TJ, SP Ilchester, for 100m. Then TR, SP Over Stratton. Pass Royal Oak pub on LHS.

4 TL, SP Wigborough/Norton sub Hamdon.
8km (5 miles)

5 TR at TJ, no SP. Enter hamlet, pass South Cottage and bear left, SP Norton sub Hamdon.

6 SO at XR, SP Norton sub Hamdon. Pass shop then Lord Nelson pub on RHS.

Food and drink

There are several pubs, shops and a tearoom in Martock, a shop in Norton sub Hamdon, and pubs and tearooms in Montecute. Refreshments are also available at Ham Hill Country Park, Montecute TV and Radio Memorabilia Museum, Montecute House and Tintinhull Garden.

Royal Oak, Over Stratton
Pub meals available.

Lord Nelson, Norton sub Hamdon
Open all day at weekends.

Prince of Wales,
Ham Hill Country Park
Serves good food. There is outside seating in a large garden.

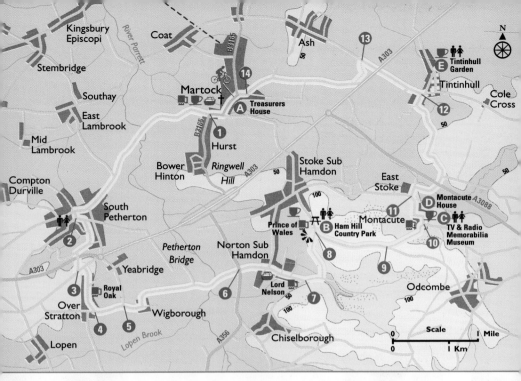

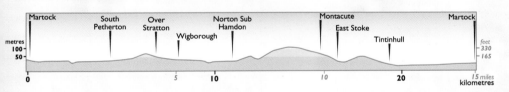

7 TL (effectively SO), SP Little Norton/
Ham Hill. Follow road as it swings left for hard
climb.

8 Reach top of hill. TL for pub/picnic area.
Otherwise, TR at TJ, no SP.

9 TL to descend along Hollow Lane, no SP.

10 TL at XR, no SP (16.5km/10.5 miles).
Pass April Cottage on LHS, then Montecute TV
and Radio Museum and Montecute House on
RHS.

11 TR, SP Tintinhull.

12 To visit Tintinhull Garden, TR at TJ and
follow SP.

Otherwise TL at TJ, SP Ash/Martock. Cross
A303 then:

13 TL, SP Martock/Ilchester. TR, SP
Martock/Yeo Paul.

14 TR along East Street, SP Martock, and
finish the ride. **24km (15 miles)**

NORTH SOMERSET COAST – WATCHET AND CLEEVE ABBEY

Route information

 Distance   26.5km (16.5 miles)

Grade   Moderate

Terrain   Mostly quiet roads with several climbs. There is one short section of A road through Williton and a short section of footpath (please walk), avoiding a busy part of the A39.

Time to allow   2–5 hours.

Getting there by car   Watchet is on the north Somerset coast. Take the A39 Bridgewater to Minehead road to Williton and then the B3191 to Watchet.

Getting there by train   There is a railway station at Watchet. Telephone (0345) 484950 for travel information.

From the attractive coastal town of Watchet the route heads west to the coastal resort of Blue Anchor. Turning inland, quiet undulating lanes take you through the attractive country-side north of the heights of Exmoor, before descending back towards the sea via the busy town of Williton and then Doniford back to Watchet.

Route description

Start from Watchet railway station and exit on town side (next to shelter). Go into Watchet along Swain Street and pass through the town bearing left by harbour entrance. Pass Market Museum on RHS. Continue out of town, climb-ing to pass several camping sites, followed by a steep descent into Blue Anchor. Pass the Blue Anchor Inn on the RHS, then Home Farm and Driftwood Café on LHS. Continue alongside sea wall to bear left and go inland.

1   SO at XR along Withycombe Lane, SP Withycombe (8km/5 miles). Climb into Withycombe.

2   TR at TJ, SP Rodhuish.

3   LHF, SP Roadwater/Washford.

4   TL at TJ, SP Washford/Roadwater.

5   TR at TJ, SP Roadwater, and descend.

6   TL at TJ, SP Hungerford/Washford.

7   To visit Cleeve Abbey, TL at TJ. Otherwise, TR at TJ, SP Monksilver/Wiveliscombe (16.5km/ 10.5 miles). Pass Torre Valley Cider Farm on LHS.

8   TL at XR onto B3190, SP Williton/Watchet/ Bridgewater. Descend.

9   TR along grass-centred lane, no SP (opposite SP Torre public footpath). Bear right at apparent TJ.

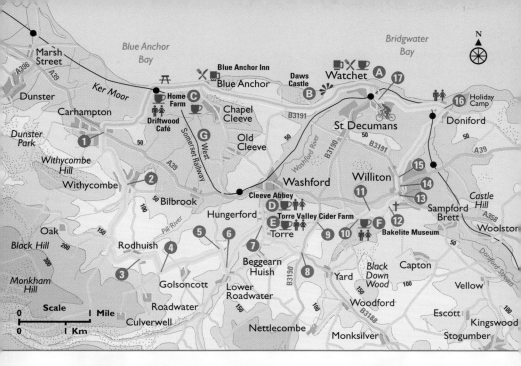

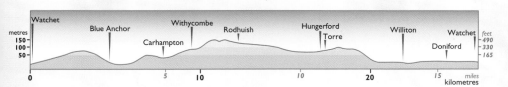

10 TL at TJ, SP Williton. Just before reaching A39:

11 TR along concrete bridleway leading into farmyard, SP yellow arrow. Pass milking parlour on RHS. Continue through gates in front to pass through yard and another gate into field. Dismount and walk along this short footpath to Bakelite Museum. Leave museum via entrance road.

12 TL at TJ, no SP. Pass church on RHS. LHF to TL at TJ, no SP.

13 TR at TJ onto A39 for 200m, no SP. TL at roundabout, SP Bridgewater/Doniford.

14 TL (effectively SO) SP Doniford/Watchet.

15 TR, SP Doniford.

16 TL at TJ, SP Watchet/Blue Anchor (24km/15 miles). Continue into Watchet.

17 TR, SP Town Centre/Harbour/Blue Anchor. Cross railway to finish the ride.

26.5km (16.5 miles)

A Watchet

The attractive harbour town of Watchet is on the north Somerset coast. Close to the harbour the varied history of the town is displayed in the **Market Museum**. Cabinets in chronological order display artefacts from mammoth teeth to Vikings, and the maritime history of this seafaring town. Open daily, summer 1030–1230 (July and August also 1900–2100); winter 1430–1630. Admission free. The **Watchet Boat Museum**, across from the station, houses the world's largest collection of Somerset Flatners, flat bottomed boats which were used extensively to carry peat and materials. Open Easter to October, Tuesday–Thursday 1100–1300, weekends 1400–1600. Admission free. Telephone (01984) 634565 for further information.

B Daws Castle, near Watchet

A few stony remains are all that is left of Daws Castle, which served as a place of refuge for the townsfolk of Watchet from Viking attack. English Heritage property. Free access at all reasonable times.

C Home Farm, Blue Anchor

Home Farm provides a wonderful opportunity to appreciate native farm animals. There are pigs, calves, donkeys and wildfowl, and lambs in spring. Café (closed Saturday). Charge. Open April to September, Sunday–Friday 1030–1730. Telephone (01984) 640817.

D Cleeve Abbey, near Washford

Founded between 1186 and 1191 the abbey is the most complete monastic settlement in Somerset. Visitors enter via a 13th-century gatehouse to see the extensive ruins featuring a Medieval painted chamber, cloisters and remarkably complete domestic buildings. English Heritage property. Small shop selling ice cream and snacks. Charge. Open daily all year, April to September 1000–1800; October 1000–1700; November to March 1000–1600. Telephone (01984) 640377.

E Torre Valley Cider Farm, Torre

Lots of animals to see, including Cynthia the Gloucester Old Spot pig and Jasmine and Hamish the Pygmy goats. Also a well-stocked farm shop specializing in local ciders and cheeses. Café. Open daily, summer 0900–1800; winter 1000–1600. Admission free. Telephone (01984) 640004.

F Bakelite Museum, near Williton.

Spanning the history of plastics from 1850 to 1950, the museum features hundreds of appliances that were once in everyday use, from irons to caravans. There is also a rural history museum featuring the work of thatchers, farmers and vets. Small café with outdoor seating. Open Easter to September, Thursday–Sunday during term time, daily during school holidays 1030–1800. Telephone (01984) 632133.

G West Somerset Railway

Spanning the countryside between Minehead and Bishops Lydeard, the West Somerset railway provides 32km (20 miles) of dedicated steam railway. Special events are held throughout summer and trains run all year round, although less frequently in winter. Telephone (01643) 704996 for details.

Food and drink

There are several places to eat in Watchet, Blue Anchor and Williton. Refreshments are also available at Home Farm, Cleeve Abbey, Torre Valley Cider Farm and the Bakelite Museum.

Blue Anchor Inn, Blue Anchor
Restaurant and pub with sea views.

THE QUANTOCK HILLS

Route information

 Distance   28km (17.5 miles)

Grade   Moderate

Terrain   A section of reasonably undemanding off-road across the Quantocks, a long on-road climb and a section of B road.

Time to allow   2–4 hours.

Getting there by car   Nether Stowey is just south of the A39 Minehead to Bridgewater road. There is a small free long-stay car park at the Quantock Hills Visitor Centre.

Getting there by train   There is no practical railway access to the ride.

Starting in Nether Stowey the route climbs quickly on sealed roads to the heights of the Quantock Hills. A glorious series of byways and bridleways cut across the top, affording extensive views of the surrounding area. Descending, again on sealed roads, to Broomfield, the highest village in the Quantocks. The route then heads north along a series of quiet lanes and returns to Nether Stowey via a B road.

Places of interest along the route

Ⓐ Nether Stowey

Nether Stowey, on the north west edge of the Quantocks, is the location of **Coleridge Cottage**, home to the poet Samuel Taylor Coleridge for three years. It was here that he wrote *The Rime of the Ancient Mariner*. The cottage is now owned by the National Trust and its two parlours are open to visitors. Open April to September, Tuesday–Thursday and Sunday 1400–1700. Charge. Telephone (01278) 732662.

Ⓑ Quantock Hills

With heavily wooded slopes and tops clothed in heathland, the Quantocks are one of Somerset's wild treasures. Extending for 19km (12 miles) from the north of Taunton, the hills were extensively used by early man as indicated by the many burial mounds. Today they are home to many species of wildlife, the most famous of which are the red deer. For further information telephone the Quantock Information Centre (see page 13).

Ⓒ Somerset Wildlife Trust, Fyne Court

Fyne Court was formerly the home of the experimental electrician Andrew Crosse, who inspired Mary Shelley to write *Frankenstein*. Today the 10.5-ha (26-acre) estate contains a walled garden, nature trails and an interpretation centre. Also shop and picnic area. Open all year, daily 0900–1800. Admission free. Telephone (01823) 451587.

Route description

Leave Quantock Visitor Centre to TL at TJ, and cycle up hill, SP Over Stowey/Crowcombe.

1 TL at TJ, no SP.

2 RHF, SP Crowcombe. Then SO at XR, SP Crowcombe (SP Dead End on RHS).

3 RHF, SP Crowcombe. Cross cattle grid and climb.

4 TL onto a wide byway, no SP (gate/style SP National Trust/Quantock Hill Footpath on LHS –if you cross a cattle grid and descend steeply you have gone 200m too far). Continue along this well defined byway through trees for 2.5km (1.5 mile). Pass car park – next turn is easy to miss. As track deteriorates to rubble there is a short climb. At top, follow much narrower track heading right (marked by small gate in fence opposite on LHS). Continue on this track for 0.5km (0.3 mile) until track joins from left. Take LHF and later another LHF (excellent views down valley on LHS). Pass through gate and continue to car park.

5 SO out of car park for descent.

6 TL at TJ (effectively SO), no SP.

7 TL at TJ, SP Enmore/Bridgewater.

8 If you do not wish to visit Somerset Wildlife Trust at Fyne Court, TL, SP Aisholt/Nether Stowey and continue on this road to direction 13. Otherwise, TR, SP Broomfield/North Petherton. Pass Pines Café/Restaurant on LHS. Continue to where road bears right:

9 To visit Fyne Court continue SO for 100m to TL, SP Broomfield/Fyne Court – Fyne Court

The Quantock Hills

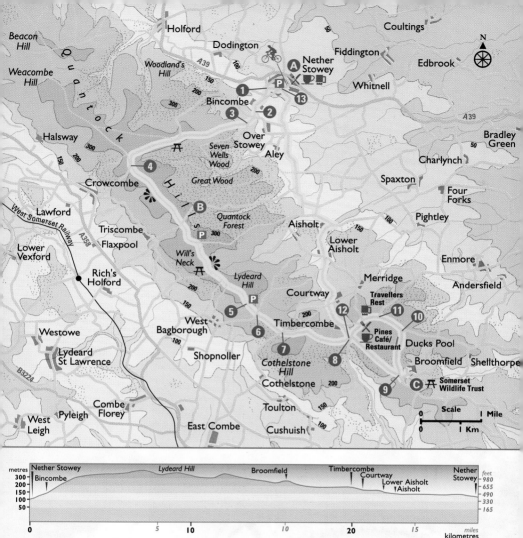

Map labels (geographic features and place names):

Beacon Hill · Weacombe Hill · Holford · Dodington · Fiddington · Coultings · Nether Stowey · Edbrook · Whitnell · Woodland's Hill · Quantock · A39 · Bincombe · Over Stowey · Aley · Halsway · Seven Wells Wood · Great Wood · Charlynch · Bradley Green · Crowcombe · Spaxton · Four Forks · Quantock Forest · Aisholt · Pightley · Lawford · West Somerset Railway · Triscombe · Flaxpool · Quantock Hills · Lower Aisholt · Enmore · Lower Vexford · Will's Neck · Merridge · Andersfield · Rich's Holford · Lydeard Hill · Courtway · Travellers Rest · Ducks Pool · Westowe · West Bagborough · Timbercombe · Pines Café/Restaurant · Broomfield · Shellthorpe · Lydeard St Lawrence · Shopnoller · Cothelstone Hill · Cothelstone · Somerset Wildlife Trust · Combe Florey · Toulton · Pyleigh · West Leigh · East Combe · Cushuish · A358 · A39 · B3324

Scale: 1 Mile / 1 Km

Elevation profile:

metres: 300, 200, 150, 100, 50
feet: 980, 655, 490, 330, 165

Nether Stowey · Bincombe · Lydeard Hill · Broomfield · Timbercombe · Courtway · Lower Aisholt · Aisholt · Nether Stowey

kilometres: 0, 5, 10, 10, 20, 15 — miles

---

entrance is 200m on LHS. Otherwise, TL along narrow shaded lane, no SP. **16km (10 miles)**

10 TL at TJ, no SP (small gravel triangle at junction).

11 TL at TJ, SP Spaxton/Bishops Lydeard/ Taunton. Pass Travellers Rest pub on RHS.

12 TR, SP Aisholt/Nether Stowey. Follow this B road back to Nether Stowey.

13 TR at TJ, SP Bridgewater/Minehead. Then TL to return to visitor centre and complete the ride. **28km (17.5 miles)**

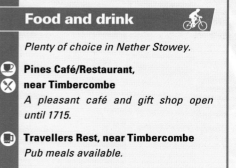

Food and drink

Plenty of choice in Nether Stowey.

Pines Café/Restaurant, near Timbercombe
A pleasant café and gift shop open until 1715.

Travellers Rest, near Timbercombe
Pub meals available.

MELKSHAM, CORSHAM AND LACOCK

Route information

 Distance   29.5km (18.5 miles)

Grade   Easy

Terrain   A few climbs and gentle gradients throughout. The section of footpath at the end of the route is commonly used by cyclists to avoid a busy road into Melksham.

Time to allow   2–3 hours.

Getting there by car   Melksham is in west Wiltshire, on the A350 south of Chippenham. There are several long-term car parks in town.

Getting there by train   There is a railway station at Melksham. Telephone (0345) 484950 for travel information.

Once a centre for the cloth trade, Melksham is now a market town and its size and railway station make a good starting point. Heading west the route passes impressive Great Chalfield Manor. Continuing north on level terrain, the route passes through Atworth before descending into Corsham. A short trip to admire the façade of Corsham Court is highly recommended before heading east to the truly delightful village of Lacock, much used as a film and television location. The route finishes along quiet lanes and a traffic-free shortcut back to Melksham.

Route description

Leave Melksham station to TL at TJ, no SP. Immediately TR at TJ (traffic lights), SP Town Centre/Bower Hill/Warminster/Devizes/Trowbridge. Continue along dual carriageway.

1   TR at large roundabout along B3107, SP Bradford/Broughton Gifford/Holt.

2   TR, SP Broughton Gifford and continue into village. Pass expansive common then Bell on the Common pub on RHS.

3   TL, SP Great Chalfield. Pass Great Chalfield Manor on RHS.

4   TR at TJ (effectively SO), SP South Wraxall/Bradford/Little Chalfield.

5   TR, SP Atworth.   ***7km (4.5 miles)***

6   TR at TJ, SP Atworth/Broughton Gifford. Continue into Atworth. Pass Forresters pub on LHS.

7   TL at TJ, SP Box. Then TR, SP Neston.

8   TR at TJ, SP Corsham/The Ridge.

9   TL along Rough Street, no SP.

10   TR at TJ, SP Corsham.

11   TL at TJ, SP Chippenham/Town Centre (16km/10 miles). Descend to SO at mini round-about and climb to:

12   To visit Corsham Court, TL at TJ and TR by Methuan Arms Hotel, walk along pedestrianised area, and continue on road to TR by Pack Horse pub. Otherwise, TR at TJ opposite iron gates, no SP. Continue along Lacock Road, descending gently. Cross railway and pass Whitehall Garden Centre on RHS.

13   SO at staggered XR (use central cycle

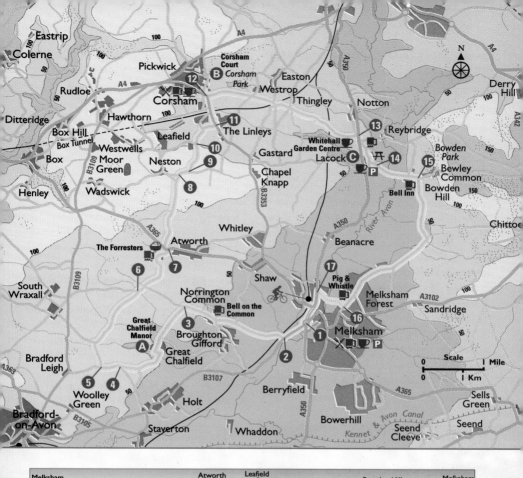

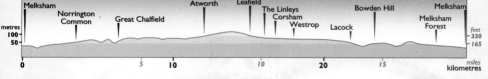

refuge). Continue along narrow path to rejoin road and enter Lacock. Pass through village and on outskirts:

14 TL at TJ opposite car park (effectively SO), no SP (22.5km/14 miles). Cross long bridge. Pass Bell Inn on RHS.

15 TR onto Forest Road, SP Melksham. Continue into Melksham. The next turn is easy to miss – pass Pig and Whistle pub on RHS, and at top of short incline:

16 TR along Murray Walk, no SP. Dismount and walk SO along footpath. Cross small footbridge and then river. Continue along street (Avon Tyres on LHS). Arrive SP for Scotland Road:

17 TL at TJ, no SP. Pass Spencer Sports and Social Club on RHS. Turn onto cyclepath (just before traffic lights) and pass under road to return to station and finish the ride.

29.5km (18.5 miles)

Places of interest along the route

A Great Chalfield Manor, Great Chalfield

Completed in 1480 and restored by Robert Fuller between 1905 and 1911, Great Chalfield Manor is a beautiful house surrounded by a moat, Elizabethan farm buildings and a church. Inside, the great hall contains a chimney piece concealing spy holes. National Trust property. Open April to October, Tuesday–Thursday 1200–1300 and 1400–1700. Visits by guided tour only. Charge.

B Corsham Court, Corsham

Originally a royal manor in the days of the Saxon kings, Corsham Court is now the home of the Methuen family. The building seen today dates from 1582 and was much altered in Georgian times. Inside is the Methuen Collection of period masks, Georgian furniture, porcelain and 16th- and 17th-century paintings.

Open March to September, Tuesday–Sunday and Bank Holiday Mondays; October to March, weekends 1400–1630. Charge. Telephone (01249) 701610.

C Lacock

The town dates from the 13th century and it's limewashed, half-timbered and stone houses have featured in many TV and film productions, including *Pride and Prejudice* and *Emma*. **Lacock Abbey**, on the outskirts of town, was founded in 1232 and converted into a country house during the 16th century. The cloisters, sacristy and monastic rooms survive almost completely intact. National Trust property. Open April to October, daily (except Tuesday afternoon) 1100–1730. Charge. Telephone (01249) 730227. The **Fox Talbot Museum** commemorates the achievements of William Fox Talbot, who invented the photographic negative and lived in the abbey. Inside there are changing exhibitions of photography. National Trust property. Open March to October, daily 1100–1730. Charge. Telephone (01249) 730459.

Lacock

Food and drink

Lots of choice in Melksham, Corsham and Lacock. There is a good shaded picnic stop outside the entrance to Lacock Abbey (through the small gate into an enclosed area).

Bell on the Common, Broughton Gifford
Bar meals available.

The Forresters, Atworth
Pub offering a wide selection of good wholesome food.

Whitehall Garden Centre, near Lacock
Purpose built tearoom serving coffee, tea and cakes all day. It does get busy at lunchtimes during weekends.

Route information

Distance   32km (20 miles)

Grade   Easy

Terrain   Cyclepaths, quiet lanes and a well-surfaced former railway line. There is one steep climb out of Glastonbury.

Time to allow   2–4 hours.

Getting there by car   Street is on the A39, Wells to Glastonbury road. Park at Clarks Village (pay and display), by the A39.

Getting there by train   There is no practical railway access to this ride.

From Street to the mystical town of Glastonbury, with its ancient abbey and alternative culture. Sustran's National Cycle Route 3 provides much of the subsequent route to Wells, via a disused railway track. The return to Street is via the flat Somerset Levels, as the route follows some of the many drainage channels that dominate the area. Note that where directions are signposted National Cycleway 3, this is indicated on the ground by a SP showing blue cycle with red number 3.

Places of interest along the route

A Street

The town owes it's success to Cyrus Clark who built a shoe factory here in 1829. **Clark's Village** is a collection of outlet stores in pleasant surroundings. Open all year, Monday–Saturday 0900–1800 (winter closes 1730), Sunday 1100-1700. The **Shoe Museum** displays shoes from Roman times to the present day, together with documents and photographs describing shoe making in Street. Open all year, Monday–Friday 1000–1645, Saturday 1000–1700, Sunday 1100–1700. Admission free. Telephone (01458) 840064.

B Glastonbury

A potent mix of Christianity and Arthurian legend are on hand in this lovely town. Towering over the area is Glastonbury Tor. Standing 159m (521 feet) above sea level it is topped by the 15th-century tower of **St Michaels Church**. Excavations here have also unearthed Dark Age and Saxon and remains. Open all year. Admission free. Telephone (01985) 843600. In the town itself lie the ruins of **Glastonbury Abbey**. Dating from the 7th century, the building has a glorious past. Three Saxon Kings were buried here and by the time of the Norman Conquest it was the wealthiest religious house in England, owning one-eighth of Somerset. Destroyed by fire in 1184 the abbey was rebuilt during the reign of Henry II, when it regained prominence until the dissolution in 1539. Today the 14.5ha (36 acres) contain extensive ruins, a visitor centre and an excellent museum of archeological finds. Open all year, daily 0930–1800 (0900 June to August). Telephone (01458) 832267. Local life is depicted in the **Somerset Rural Life Museum**, which brims with relics of everything from cider making to peat digging. Housed in the Abbey Barn the museum is open Easter to October, Monday–Friday 1000–1700, weekends 1400-1800. Charge. Telephone (01458) 831197.

ⓒ Wells

Wells is a compact city, full of fascinating sights. Originally dating from the 13th century, the **Bishops Palace** is the residence of the Bishop of Bath and Wells. The gatehouse entrance has a portcullis and chute which was used for pouring boiling oil and molten lead. Inside, the palace and grounds are surrounded by a moat fed by the springs, or wells, after which the city is named. Tearoom. Open Easter to October, Tuesday–Friday 1030–1800, Sunday 1400–1800 (also Bank Holiday Mondays and daily in August). Charge. Telephone (01749) 678691. The fully restored West Front depicting the Last Judgement is one of the many features of **Wells Cathedral**. Built during the 12th and 13th centuries, the cathedral was the first completely English gothic cathedral. Extensive lawns at the front are ideal for a picnic. Admission by donation. Guided tours available. Open daily from 0715. Telephone (01749) 674483. **Wells Museum** provides a fascinating insight into the local life and legends of Wells and the surrounding Mendips. Open Easter to October, daily 1000–1730 (July and August closes 2000); November to Easter, Wednesday–Sunday 1100–1600. Charge. Telephone (01749) 673477.

Route description

Start from Tourist Information Centre in centre of Clarke's Village. Walk through metal columned arcade away from central square, following SP High Street shops. TL at road, SP High Street shops. Follow this road to TL at XR, SP Shoe Museum, passing museum on LHS. Take second exit at roundabout along Church Road, SP Strode Campus, passing to left of Street Inn. Pass close to Holy Trinity Church on LHS and TR into Bowling Green (street name) at mini roundabout. A fine view of Glastonbury Tor opens up on LHS.

1 TL at XR, no SP. Cross stone bridge and just after SP 30MPH:

2 TR along Old Butleigh Road, no SP. Climb.

3 TR at TJ to visit Somerset Rural Life Museum. Otherwise, TL at TJ, no SP (4km/2.5 miles). Follow road as it bears right, SP Bridgwater/Taunton. SO at roundabout, SP Town Centre/Abbey. Pass abbey on RHS to bear right and climb, passing shops and cafés.

4 SO at XR, SP National Cycleway 3. Climb for a lovely view of Mendips.

5 TR just before main road (A39), onto cyclepath that runs parallel to main road, SP National Cycleway 3.

6 TR at TJ, SP Launcherley (8km/5 miles). Continue along this straight, flat road, passing distinctive Sustran markers on LHS.

7 TL at TJ, SP National Cycleway 3.

8 SO at XR, SP National Cycleway 3. Climb.

9 TR, SP National Cycleway 3.

10 TL at TJ for 100m, SP Wells/Shepton Mallett/Frome. TR, SP National Cycleway 3, passing under road to TL onto track, SP Wells. Track joins disused railway. Unsealed surface eventually turns into tarmac path next to road. When cycle path ends, SP Cyclists Dismount:

11 To visit Wells, TR at roundabout, passing Sherston Inn on RHS. As this road swings left, TR (effectively SO) and continue SO. After short distance road becomes one way – walk along shop-lined street to visit cathedral and other attractions.

Otherwise, to continue route, SO at roundabout along Strawberry Way, SP Bath/Cheddar.

16.5km (10.5 miles)

12 TL at XR (traffic lights), along Burcott Road. Exit city and continue along narrow, green lane for 3km (2 miles). Then bear right opposite SP Unsuitable for Heavy Goods Vehicles.

13 TL at TJ (next to Pine Tree Farm), no SP. Follow SP Godney/Glastonbury.

14 TL at XR, SP Godney/Glastonbury (24km/15 miles). Pass under high power cables.

15 SO at XR, SP Glastonbury (World War II

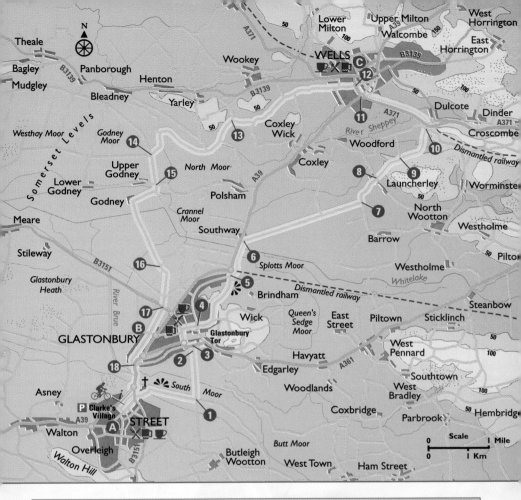

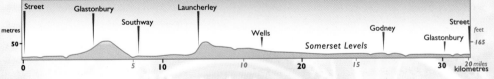

defensive bunker on RHS). Continue through village and just after Sweet Acre Nursery:

16 TR at TJ, no SP. Cross bridge and immediately TL, passing SP Width Restriction.

17 SO at mini roundabout, SP Public Weighbridge. SO at second mini roundabout, SP Street. Pass through industrial estate.

18 TR (just before main road) onto narrow cycle path, no SP. Follow cycle path, crossing road once. At large roundabout join A39 for short distance to return to Clark's village and the end of the ride. **32km (20 miles)**

Food and drink

Plenty of choice in Street and Clark's Village, Glastonbury and Wells.

BATH, LANSDOWN AND BITTON

Route information

Distance 33km (20.5 miles)

Grade Strenuous

Terrain Tarmac roads and a tarmac cycle path that is a little rough right at the end. One long climb and several short, sharp climbs.

Time to allow 3–5 hours.

Getting there by car There are several long-stay car parks in Bath. Free parking is available at the west end of Royal Victoria Park.

Getting there by train The nearest railway station is Bath Spa station. Telephone (0345) 484950 for travel information.

Starting from the railway station, the route winds its way through Bath passing several of the famous attractions. A steep climb takes you up and over Lansdown, the effort rewarded with fine views and a descent to the picturesque village of Doynton. On south through the Golden Valley to join the Sustrans Bristol & Bath Railway Path, which provides a flat and scenic ride back to Bath.

Places of interest along the route

Ⓐ Bath

Renowned as a World Heritage City, Bath has many attractions for the visitor. The highlights include: Royal Crescent, designed by John Wood the Younger; No. 1 Royal Crescent, restored to its original Georgian splendour and open to the public; the Roman Baths, renovated by the Victorians; the Pump Room, where visitors can taste the tepid spa water; and Bath Abbey and the restored 18th-century vaults. There are also many museums, including: Bath Postal Museum; the Museum of Costume and Assembly Rooms; Holborne Museum; the American Museum and Gardens; Sally Lunn's Refreshment House and Museum; and the Bath Industrial Heritage Centre. There is a Victorian Boating Station and visitors can take boat trips on the Kennet & Avon Canal. Telephone the Tourist Information Centre for further details on (01225) 477101.

Ⓑ Beckfords Tower, Lansdown Park

Climb the 156 steps up Beckfords Tower for wonderful vistas of Bath. The small museum at the base of the tower includes information on Beckford himself. National Lottery funding has enabled the entire building to be renovated to its original state. Open April to October, weekends and Bank Holiday Mondays 1400–1700. Charge. Telephone (01225) 312917.

Ⓒ Sir Bevil Grenville's Monument, near Wick

Marking the site of the civil war battle of Lansdown Hill, fought on 5 July 1643, the monument is in memory of this Royalist officer killed during in battle. Free access at all reasonable times.

Ⓓ Avon Valley Railway, Bitton Station

The Avon Valley Railway is run by enthusiasts. Steam trains are run regularly at weekends in summer. There is a shop and museum on site. Also tearoom with outside seating. Free admission to the station, charge for train rides.

Telephone (0117) 9327296 for the talking timetable; (0117) 9325538 for weekend enquiries.

E Bristol and Bath Railway Path

The first section of the Sustrans National Cycle Route (NCR) is widely known as the Bristol & Bath Railway Path. Tarmacked along much of its length, the path provides a safe corridor for pedestrians, cyclists and horse riders between Bristol and Bath. Over one million journeys are made each year along it's 20km (12.5 mile) length. Free access at all times.

Roman Baths, Bath

Route description

Leave Bath Spa station to head past Royal Hotel (RHS) and bus station (LHS), initially walking first 20m. SO at traffic lights to bear left, past Bath Abbey on LHS. Immediately bear left (in front of church) to pass Guildhall on RHS. Climb past Postal Museum on LHS. TL at XR (traffic lights), SP Bristol/Hospital. Follow road as it bears left after 400m. Continue for 20m and TR along Queen's Parade Place to enter Royal Victoria Park between two pillars. Cycle through park admiring Royal Crescent on RHS.

1 TR at XR along Marlborough Buildings, no SP (Royal Crescent still on RHS). SO at XR along Cavendish Road, no SP, past Approach Golf Course on LHS. Start hard climb. SO at XR along Winifred's Lane (telephone RHS) and climb this narrow lane.

2 TR at TJ into Sion Road, no SP.

3 TL at XR opposite Northfields, no SP. Continue climbing, passing several schools on either side of road. Road starts to flatten by pub. Continue, admiring extensive views on LHS. Pass Hare and Hounds pub on RHS, Beckfords Tower on LHS, then Greville's Monument on RHS. Continue for fast descent past Tracy Park on RHS.

4 SO at XR along London Road, SP Doynton/Dyrham (11km/7 miles). Enter Doynton.

5 TL, SP Abson/Pucklechurch. Pass Cross House pub on RHS.

6 TL, SP Abson/Pucklechurch.

7 TL at XR along Naishcombe Hill.
16km (10 miles)

8 TL at TJ for 20m, SP Chippenham. TL at TJ, no SP. Pass Carpenters Arms pub LHS.

9 Easy to miss – TR into Manor Road, no SP (if you pass Rose and Crown pub, you have gone too far).

10 TL at TJ, no SP. *17.5km (11 miles)*

11 TR, SP Upton Cheyney/Bitton.

12 TR at TJ, SP (on wall) Bitton.

13 TR at TJ onto A431, SP Bristol. Pass White Hart pub on LHS, then shops/Post Office on RHS.

14 TR, SP Avon Valley Railway (22km/13.5 miles). Gently climb to car park and onto cycle path to left of station. Cross level crossing to continue along tarmac (railway on LHS). Pass Bird in Hand pub on RHS.

At end of path, pass through barrier, cross red tarmac and continue along street, returning to riverside at SP No Entry. Continue along path following river, SP City Centre. Path ends and SO, past multi-storey car park on LHS. Bear right (by Quasar) and bear left (by Boots) along Dorchester Street. Follow this road past bus station to railway station and the end of the ride. *33km (20.5 miles)*

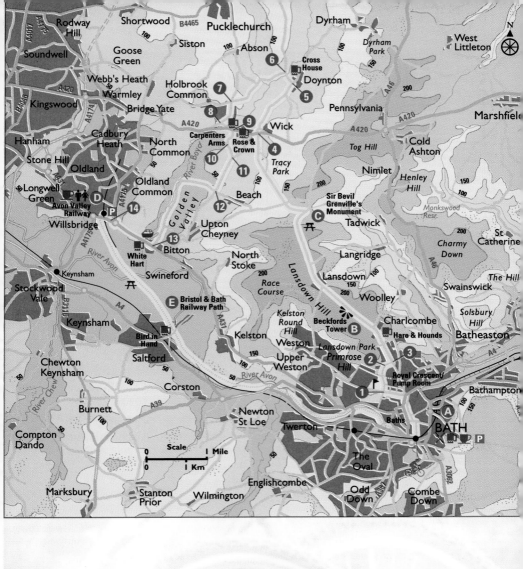

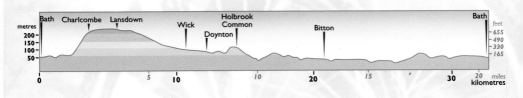

CHISELDON, AVEBURY AND MARLBOROUGH

Route information

Distance   43km (27 miles)

Grade   Moderate

Terrain   An off-road section along the Ridgeway, tarmac road and converted railway path give plenty of variety.

Time to allow   3–6 hours.

Getting there by car   The route starts in Chiseldon. Take junction 15 from the M4, towards Marlborough. After 1.5km (1 mile) just after garage, TR SP HGV Testing Station. Park in the small car park at the end of the railway path, 100m on LHS.

Getting there by train   There is no practical railway access to this ride.

This route takes in three distinct terrains. From Chiseldon you head off-road along the Ridgeway, through Barbury Castle. Then a descent takes you towards the awe inspiring stones at Avebury. On-road through Avebury and into Marlborough via the Kennet valley. The final section of the route follows a traffic free railway path, built by Sustrans and maintained by local volunteers.

Places of interest along the route

A **Barbury Castle, Marlborough Downs**
The castle is on one of the highest points on the downs. It was built by the Celts in the 6th century

BC and acted as a refuge against warring tribes. The castle originally consisted of two banks – the inner held a continuous wooden fence whilst the outer was reinforced with huge sandstone blocks. The area covers 4.5ha (11.5 acres) and excavation has revealed weapons, tools and chariot equipment. Picnic area with fine views. Free access at all reasonable times. Telephone Swindon Countryside Ranger for further information on (01793) 771419.

B **Avebury**
The great **stone circle** at Avebury encompasses part of the village and is enclosed by a ditch and bank. The circle itself is approached by an avenue of stones. Many of the stones were re-erected in the 1930s by the archaeologist Alexander Keiller. National Trust property. Free access at all reasonable times. Much of Avebury's history is explained in the **Alexander Keiller Museum**. Founded in 1938, it contains a record of the excavation of the stone circle during the late 1920s and 1930s and holds one of the country's most important archeological collections. National Trust property. Open daily, summer 1000–1800; winter 1000–1600. Charge. Telephone (01672) 539250. The **Great Barn Museum** is devoted to life in Wiltshire. It is housed in a 17th-century thatched barn and contains a wide range of agricultural equipment. Also rural craft demonstrations and a local produce shop. Open daily, mid-March to mid-November 1000–1730. Charge. Telephone (01672) 539555. **Avebury Manor** is of monastic origin, and the present building dates from the early 16th century, with Queen Anne alterations and Edwardian renovations. Privately occupied National Trust property. Open April to October, Tuesday, Wednesday, Sunday and Bank

Holiday Mondays 1400–1730. Charge. Telephone (01672) 539250.

Ⓒ Marlborough

King Arthur's magician Merlin is reputedly buried under a mound here, so giving Marlborough its original name of Merle Barrow. Today the town has one of the widest high streets in England, with many Georgian buildings and architectural styles spanning 300 years. Away from the centre there are older timber-framed buildings that survived three fires during the 17th century. The Mop Fair takes place in the High Street over two weekends each October.

Ⓓ Chiseldon and Marlborough Railway Path

Constructed and maintained by Sustrans, the path provides 12km (7.5 miles) of safe cycling as an alternative to the busy A346. The surface is well-graded although a little narrow in places due to vegetation. Free access at all times.

Food and drink

Avebury has a pub and a small store. There is also a store in West Overton, a pub at Manton and plenty of choice in Marlborough.

Frog & Spoon, Barbury Castle
Delightful café with only outdoor seating, where you can purchase teas, ice creams and limited bicycle spares. Camping available. Open every weekend throughout the year and daily in summer.

Stones Restaurant, Avebury
Offers wonderful wholesome cakes and meals.

The Man Who'd a Thought It, near West Overton
Food available. Beer garden. Closed Mondays.

Avebury stone circle

Route description

Start from the small car park at the end of the railway path in Chiseldon. Exit to TL at TJ, no SP, passing New Farm Cottages on LHS. As road bears left:

1 TR at a triangular grassed junction, no SP. Pass wooden SP Barbury Castle via Old Ridgeway then buildings on RHS and continue onto a firmer track.

2 TL at TJ onto tarmac, no SP, and start hard climb. *4km (2.5 miles)*

3 TR, SP Barbury Castle Country Park Car Park. Follow road into car park to bear left past toilets, through gate into eastern entrance of castle. Descend once through western entrance.

4 TR at TJ, SP Ridgeway. Then TL, SP Ridgeway, onto off-road.

5 SO at XR, SP Ridgeway (firm off-road which later becomes longitudinally rutted but is still cycleable). *9.5km (6 miles)*

6 TR, SP Byway (opposite SP Fyfield Down National Nature Reserve). Descend, eventually rejoining tarmac.

7 TL (effectively SO) at TJ, no SP but opposite Red Lion (16km/10 miles). To visit Avebury Manor and Stones Restaurant TR after 20m.

8 TL (effectively SO), no SP. Follow avenue of stones on RHS. Enter West Kennett.

9 TL at TJ onto A4, SP Marlborough.

10 TR, SP East Kennett/Woodborough. Enter East Kennett.

11 TL, SP West Overton. Continue through West Overton and into Lockeridge.

12 TL for The Man Who'd a Thought It pub. Otherwise, TR at TJ, SP Alton Barnes/ Woodborough. Then TL, no SP (pass SP Unsuitable for Heavy Goods Vehicles).

13 TL at TJ, no SP (24km/15 miles). Pass Bankside (house name) on RHS. Continue through Clatford and Manton. Pass Oddfellow Arms on LHS and:

14 TR, no SP (26.5km/16.5 miles). Pass wooden village hall on LHS, SP Dead End and just after large red building on LHS:

15 RHF, no SP (27km/17 miles), to bear left onto track passing tennis courts on RHS, SP 4. Continue on path, keeping stream on LHS. Pass through gate.

16 SO at XR along George Lane, no SP.

17 TL along Figgins Lane, SP Council Offices. Cycle through car park, past Tourist Information Centre on RHS. Cross bridge and continue SO, walking last 20m through arch.

18 TR at TJ along wide High Street, no SP.

19 TR at large roundabout, SP Salisbury/ Hungerford.

20 TL, SP Hungerford/London.

21 TL along Elcot Lane, SP Chiseldon and Marlborough Railway Path. As road narrows, SO passing Roselea (house name) on RHS. Continue under bridge and immediately TR, SP Chiseldon and Marlborough Railway Path. Climb gently for 100m to TR onto railway path. Follow path northwards. Where you arrive at tarmac again:

22 TL at TJ, no SP (37.5km/23.5 miles). Pass Foxlynch (house name) on RHS.

23 TL at XR, SP Ogbourne St George. Continue under road to TR back onto path.

24 TR at TJ onto tarmac for 75m, no SP. through green bollards, back onto path and continue into car park to finish the ride.

43km (27 miles)

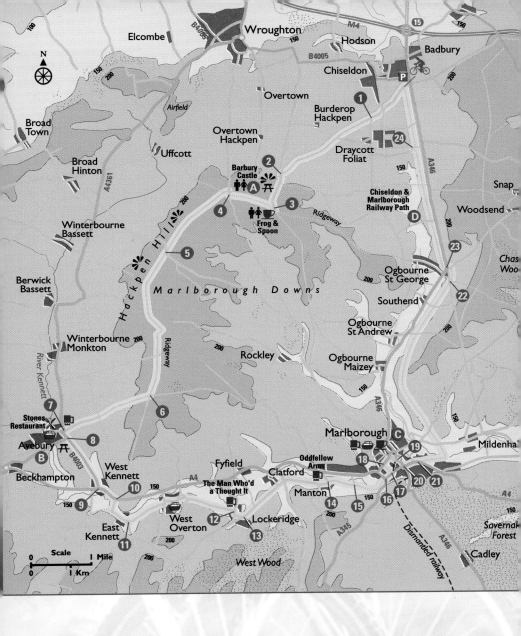

N

Elcombe
Wroughton
M4
Hodson
Badbury
15
B4005
Chiseldon
P
Overtown
Burderop
Hackpen
1
Airfield
Overtown
Hackpen
Draycott
Foliat
24
150
Broad
Town
Barbury
Castle
2
A
Uffcott
Chiseldon &
Marlborough
Railway Path
Snap
Broad
Hinton
A4361
3
Ridgeway
D
Woodsend
4
Frog &
Spoon
23
Winterbourne
Bassett
200
5
Ogbourne
St George
Chas
Woo
Berwick
Bassett
Marlborough Downs
200
Southend
22
Hackpen Hill
200
Ogbourne
St Andrew
Winterbourne
Monkton
200
Ridgeway
200
Rockley
Ogbourne
Maizey
200
River Kennett
6
150
A345
200
7
Stones
Restaurant
Marlborough
C
Mildenha
Avebury
8
B4003
19
West
Kennett
Fyfield
Oddfellow
Arms
18
20 21
B
Clatford
17
Beckhampton
10
150
A4
The Man Who'd
a Thought It
Manton
16
A4
9
150
150
West
Overton
14
Savernal
Forest
East
Kennett
12
Lockeridge
15
200
Dismantled railway
150
11
13
A345
A346
Cadley
200
West Wood
Scale
1 Mile
1 Km

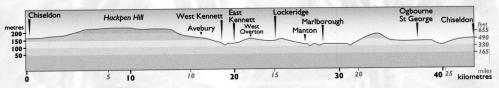

metres
200
150
100
50

Chiseldon   Hackpen Hill   West Kennett   East   Lockeridge   Ogbourne   Chiseldon
                              Avebury   Kennett   Marlborough   St George
                                         West   Manton
                                         Overton

feet
655
490
330
165

0   5   10   10   20   15   30   20   40 25   kilometres
                                                              miles

51

SWINDON AND THE COTSWOLD WATER PARK

Route information

Distance   48km (30 miles)

Grade   Easy

Terrain   Generally quiet undulating and flat roads and a section of tarmac cycleway.

Time to allow   3–5 hours.

Getting there by car   Take junction 16 from the M4 towards Swindon and follow brown SP to Lydiard Park.

Getting there by train   The nearest railway station is in Swindon. Lydiard Park is on the west side of Swindon. Telephone Swindon Tourist Information Centre on (01793) 530328 for the excellent free *Swindon Cycle Map and Guide.*

From Lydiard Park the ride heads north west to the Cotswold Water Park. The water park was created from a large number of flooded gravel pits and the routes takes you past several of these to the attractive village of Ashton Keynes. East from here to pass a preserved railway line, before returning to Lydiard Park via a series of cycleways.

Places of interest along the route

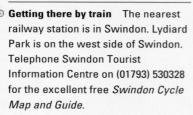

A Lydiard House and Park, Swindon
Rescued from ruin in 1943, Lydiard House was the ancestral home of the Viscounts

Bolingbroke. The ground floor is open to the public and contains original family furniture set amongst ornate plasterwork. Surrounding the house is Lydiard Park, containing an ice house, lake and children's adventure playground. Paths throughout the woods provide glimpses of wildlife whilst the lawns make good places to picnic. The Visitor Centre contains country-side displays and a café. House (admission charge) open all year, Monday–Friday 1000–1300 and 1400–1700, Saturday 1000–1700, Sunday 1400–1700 (November to February closed 1600). Grounds (admission free) open all year, 0730–dusk. Telephone (01793) 770401.

B Purton Museum, Purton
Situated in the library, the museum has displays on local history, including Neolithic flints and shards of pottery from Purton's roman kilns as well as agricultural hand tools and dairy equipment. Open all year, Tuesday 1400–1700 and 1800–2000, Wednesday 1000–1300 and 1400–1700, Friday 1400–1700 and 1800–2000. Admission free. Telephone (01793) 770567.

C Neigh Bridge, Cotswold Country Park
Neigh Bridge is part of the extensive Cotswold Water Park. This pleasant lakeside area is equipped with a children's play area and picnic tables. Access free all year (toilets summer only).

D Swindon and Cricklade Railway
This railway uses the old trackbed of the Midland and South Western Junction Railway. Restoration began in 1979 and at present the railway comprises 400m of track along which several locomotives, including steam engines, are run. Future plans include a considerable extension of track, but for now you can enjoy watching the restoration work, visiting the

museum and sampling the snacks on offer. Open every weekend throughout the year, 1000–1600. Telephone (01793) 771615 weekends; (01793) 870773 weekdays.

Route description

Leave the car park at Lydiard Park via exit.

1 TR at TJ, no SP. Cycle along this single track road with passing places. Enter Hook.

2 TR at TJ, SP Purton. Pass Bolingbroke Arms on RHS. Continue through Greatfield (Butchers Arms pub on LHS) and into Restrop the Purton. As road bears right by shops:

3 To visit Purton Museum, continue SO for 0.3km (0.5 mile) for a gentle descent – museum is on LHS. Otherwise, to continue route TL along Pavenhill, no SP, for descent with good views.

4 SO at XR, SP Minety (9.5km/6 miles). Continue into Minety.

5 SO at XR along Silver Street, SP Minety.

6 TR, SP Somerford Keynes/Ashford Keynes (14.5km/9 miles). Continue along Sawyers Hill.

7 SO at XR, SP Somerford Keynes. Pass entrance to Neigh Bridge Country Park on LHS. Enter Somerford Keynes.

8 To visit Bakers Arms, continue SO for 40m. Otherwise, TR, SP Ashton Keynes/Cricklade.

9 TR at TJ, SP Poole Keynes/Minety. Then TL at TJ, SP Ashton Keynes.

10 TR at XR, SP Wootton Bassett/Ashton Keynes/Minety. Enter Ashton Keynes.

11 TL along Cox's Hill, SP Ashton Keynes.

12 TL along Back Street, no SP.

13 TR at TJ along Rixon Gate, no SP.

14 TL at TJ, no SP (24km/15 miles). Pass Inauda (house name) on RHS and leave village.

15 SO at XR, SP Chelworth.

16 SO at XR (staggered) no SP. Cross small bridge.

17 TL to visit Swindon and Cricklade Railway. Otherwise, SO at XR, SP West Swindon/Lydiard Millicent. *33km (20.5 miles)*

18 TR by Foresters Arms, SP Lydiard Millicent. Just before arriving at TJ (TL SP Swindon):

19 TL, SP Link Centre/Swindon Centre (blue cycleway SP), and follow cycleway for 200m to cross Middleleaze Drive. After further 100m take RHF to pass through tunnel under road. TL at TJ, no SP (ignore TL over bridge with metal railings). Cross small stone bridge to continue along cycleway (keeping houses on LHS, fields RHS). Arrive at road and TR, SP Lydiard Park Conference Centre. Descend into park, bear left (to the right of church) past conference centre entrance on LHS. Pass through gate and walk along path through the woods, passing Forest Café on RHS. Continue into car park to complete the ride. *48km (30 miles)*

Food and drink

Refreshments are available at Lydiard Park and Swindon and Cricklade Railway.

Bakers Arms, Somerford Keynes
Pub meals available. Also garden with seating and children's play area.

Foresters Arms, Common Platt
Hot and cold bar snacks and a beer garden.

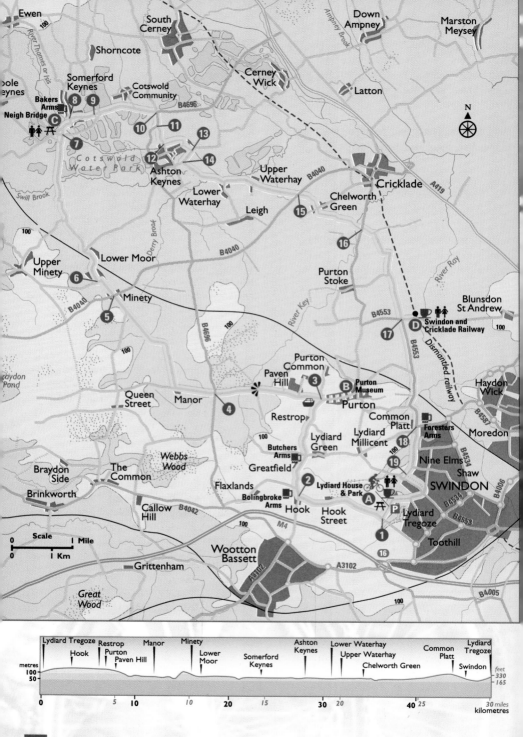

MALMESBURY AND CASTLE COMBE

Route information

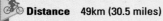

Distance   49km (30.5 miles)

Grade   Easy

Terrain   Tarmac road and the Fosse Way, which is interspersed with sections suitable only for a mountain bike and can be sticky in places when the weather is wet.

Time to allow   3–5 hours.

Getting there by car   Malmesbury is close to the Wiltshire/ Gloucestershire border. Take the A429 north from junction 17 of the M4. There is long-term car parking in town.

Getting there by train   There is no practical railway access to this ride.

From Malmesbury, the route follows the River Avon valley through the attractive village of Sherston into Luckington. Southwards to beautiful Castle Combe. The route now follows the ancient Fosse Way as it passes as straight as an arrow through the verdant countryside. Much of this section is off-road and varies from a narrow hedged track to a wide expansive byway, where you may be joined by off-road vehicles. The Fosse Way is left to the north of Malmesbury and a quiet lane via Charlton takes you back to the start.

Places of interest along the route

Ⓐ Malmesbury

Claiming to be the oldest borough in England, Malmesbury is perched on top of a hill. **Malmesbury Abbey** dates from the 12th century. By the 14th century it was an enormous structure, reaching 97.5m (320 feet) in length. A storm in 1479 brought down the spire, and the Dissolution of the Abbeys in 1539 brought further destruction. However, the remains include one of the finest Romanesque stone carvings in Britain, depicting the apostles. Open all year, daily 1000-1600 by donation. Adjoining the abbey is the **Abbey Parvis Museum**. The collection illustrates much of the abbey's past and includes a 12th-century manuscript written in Anglo-Norman, Roman and medieval tiles as well as the organ from 1714. Opening times as per the abbey. Telephone (01666) 822075. Local history is depicted in the **Athelstan Museum**, situated in the town hall. The collection includes such diverse items as lace and early bicycles as well as an 18th-century manual fire engine. Open Easter to September, Tuesday to Sunday. Telephone (01666) 22143.

Ⓑ Castle Combe

Widely acknowledged as one of the prettiest villages in England. Visitors can see the 13th-century market cross and a pack bridge across the stream which runs through the centre of the village. For a land locked place, Castle Combe received international recognition as a seaport in *Dr Doolittle* which was filmed here in

Castle Combe

1966. Close to the village is **Castle Combe Circuit** which hosts 12 motor race meetings a year. Also skid pan and kart track. Telephone (01249) 783010 for further details.

Fosse Way

The Fosse Way is an ancient trackway adapted by the Romans and still largely followed by present-day roads. It runs from near Sidmouth in Devon to the Humber, by Ilchester, Leicester and Lincoln, where it meets the Roman Ermine Street.

Food and drink

There is plenty of choice in Malmesbury. Sherston has two pubs, a post office and convenience store. There is also a post office and stores in Luckington.

Royal Ship, Luckington
A 17th-century pub offering food.

Salutation Inn, The Gib
Bar meals available.

Route description

Start in the centre of Malmesbury at the town hall (which incorporate the Tourist Information Centre). From the adjacent short stay car park enter the one way system (skirts car park), to pass red telephone box on RHS. TR at TJ, SP Long Stay Car Park, passing Lloyds Bank and then Kings Arms Hotel on LHS. TL at TJ along Gloucester Street (opposite market cross and Whole Hog Eatery). Pass large mirror on LHS and bear right, subsequently passing Abbey on RHS.

1 TL at TJ (opposite large stone cross) for 200m, no SP. Then TR along Foxley Road, SP Foxley. Continue through Foxley.

2 SO at XR, SP Luckington/Sherston.

3 TR along lane with wood on LHS and low wall on RHS, no SP but just past SP bridleway on LHS (8km/5 miles). Descend to:

4 TR at TJ, SP Sherston/Tetbury. Cross bridge and climb.

5 TL at XR, SP Luckington/Chipping

Sodbury/Bristol. Continue through Sherston (no SP) and Luckington.

6 TL, SP Alderton.

7 TR at XR, SP Littleton Drew.

8 TL at TJ, no SP (17.5km/11 miles). Continue through Littleton Drew (no SP) and under M4.

9 TL at TJ, SP Chippenham/Castle Combe. Pass Salutation Inn on LHS.

10 To visit Castle Combe, TR following SP. Otherwise, TL, SP Grittleton.

11 TL at TJ, SP Luckington/Alderton/Grittleton. Cross M4 and enter Grittleton.

12 SO at XR, SP Alderton/Luckington/Sherston (24km/15 miles). When road bears right and continues SO, you are on Fosse Way.

13 SO at XR (by red post box on RHS), SP Byway. Continue along this wide byway.

14 TL (effectively SO) at TJ back onto tarmac for 400m, no SP. As road bears left:

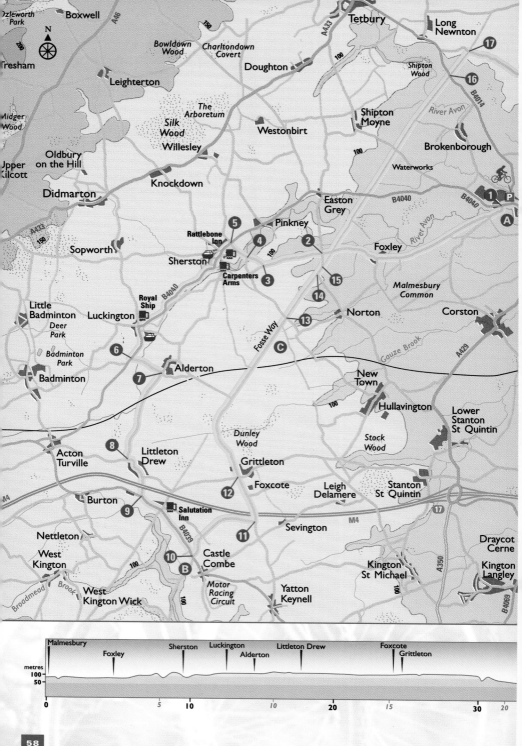

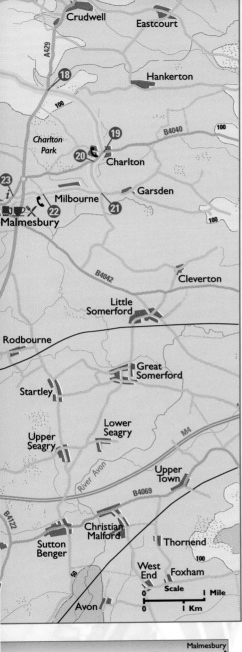

15 TR along hedge lined track, SP Byway (31.5km/19.5 miles). When you reach tarmac continue SO, SP Byway. Continue on byway to descend and cross three-arched stone bridge over River Avon. Cross another road, SP Byway, to pass Skipton Moyne Waterworks on LHS. Cross another road, passing Fosse Cottages on RHS. After this byway becomes tarmac. As tarmac bears right, continue SO passing SP warning of ford for four-wheel drive vehicles. Cross ford via bridge (for foot and two-wheeled traffic only) to climb to:

16 SO at XR, no SP but Gloucestershire/ Cotswold District SP on LHS. Follow byway. At junction (with agricultural buildings on RHS):

17 TR at XR, no SP but red PFT SP on other side (38.5km/24 miles). Surface becomes tarmac.

18 SO at XR across A429, SP Charlton Lea. Continue along this road with passing places into Charlton.

19 TR at TJ (telephone box RHS), SP Malmesbury.

20 TL, SP Garsden Lea.

21 TR at XR, SP Milbourne/Malmesbury. Enter Milbourne.

22 TL (effectively SO) next to red telephone box, SP Wiltshire Cycleway (48km/30 miles). Cross A429 to descend Blicks Hill.

23 TL at TJ opposite Duke of York pub, no SP. Cross River Avon and climb back into Malmesbury to complete the route.

49km (30.5 miles)

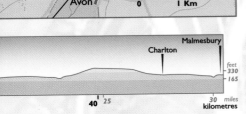

ASHTON COURT AND CLEVEDON

Route information

Distance   51.5km (32 miles)

Grade   Moderate

Terrain   Level cycling on-road throughout most of the route. The last 9.5km (6 miles) contain several climbs but only one is long.

Time to allow   3-6 hours.

Getting there by car   The route starts at Ashton Court. From the map it appears to have several entrances but only one allows access to the mansion and car park. From the A369, follow SP Ashton Court. There is a free car park 200m past the entrance.

Getting there by train   There is no railway station at Ashton Court. However, there is a station at Yatton. To join the route, exit the station to TL at TJ and join the route at direction 13.

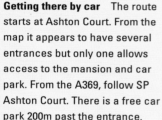

From the imposing structure of Ashton Court, the route wends its way out of the park and through Long Ashton. The flat route takes you through the pretty villages of Backwell and Claverham to Yatton. More flat riding ensues as you head north west to Clevedon, where the pier and a breath of sea air are the reward. On eastwards through the Gordano Valley with the M5 high above to the right, along one of the loveliest roads in the area. The route then takes a more elevated view as it climbs to Failand. The final section takes you through woodland back to Ashton Court.

Places of interest along the route

Ⓐ Ashton Court

Only 3km (2 miles) from the centre of Bristol, Ashton Court is a country park set in 344ha (850 acres) of woods and grassland. Central to the park is the mansion. Originally constructed in Medieval times, it was gradually extended by the Smyth family until its acquisition in 1959 by Bristol City Council. Today it serves as a centre for wedding receptions and seminars. Monthly tours are available, telephone (0117) 963 3438 for information. Adjacent to the house are the old stables, now a visitor centre providing information on local history and wildlife and a café. The park itself is criss-crossed with paths, some of which are marked for mountain bikes. As well as oak trees and a lime avenue there are deer in enclosures and extensive views across Clifton to the hills beyond. Free Access. Special events such as balloon festivals and the North Somerset Show are held throughout the year. Telephone (0117) 963 9174. Free admission to the park at all reasonable times.

B Clevedon

Clevedon was originally an agricultural village but has grown enormously since building plots along the beach were first advertised in 1820. Today it is a busy seaside town. The pier, built in 1869, is one of only three piers that are grade 2 listed. During load testing for insurance in 1970, the end section of the pier collapsed and was not reopened until 1989. Today, for a small fee, you can walk the promenade. Telephone (01275) 878846. **Clevedon Court** is an outstanding 14th-century manor house, incorporating a massive 12th-century tower and 13th-century great hall. There is also a terraced garden dating from the 18th century. National Trust property. Tearoom. Open March to September, Wednesday, Thursday, Sunday and Bank Holiday Mondays 1400–1700. Charge. Telephone (01275) 872257.

Food and drink

Plenty of choice in Long Ashton, Yatton and Clevedon. Also pubs in Backwell Farleigh and convenience stores in Claverham. Refreshments are also available at Ashton Court and Clevedon Court.

Jubilee Inn, Flax Bourton
The pub celebrates Queen Victoria's Jubilee and sports a garden away from the road.

Round Trees Garden Centre, Yatton
Traditional teashop located in the garden centre.

Prince of Orange, Yatton
Offering meals. There is a large CTC plaque bolted to the outside wall.

Route description

Start from Ashton Court visitor centre (behind mansion house). Exit short drive to TL at TJ, no SP, continue past mansion house on LHS and through car park. Take LHF, SP Long Ashton, to descend and pass through gatehouse.

1   SO at XR, no SP, and immediately enter Long Ashton.

2   SO at XR (double mini roundabout) SP Farleigh Hospital/Magistrates court. Descend passing Woodspring Magistrates Court on RHS. As road bears right (with church on RHS):

3   TL along dead end road that ends at short cycleway, no SP (4.5km/3 miles). TR at TJ, no SP, immediately entering Flax Bourton. Continue through village and into Backwell Farleigh. Pass George pub on RHS and:

4   TL along Church Lane, no SP. Climb, passing church on RHS. Road swings right, pass TL (Church Town) and:

5   TL along Church Lane No. 74–112, no SP.
9km (5.5 miles)

6   TL at TJ, no SP. Pass New Inn on RHS and Rising Sun on LHS.

7   TR, SP Chelvey/Clevedon.
10.5km (6.5 miles)

8   TL, broken SP, and pass Chestnut Cottage on RHS.

9   TL at TJ for 100m, no SP. TR along Brockley Way, SP Claverham/Yatton. Just before passing under high voltage cables:

10   TL along Brockley Way, no SP.
14.5km (9 miles)

11   TR at TJ along Claverham Road, no SP.

12   To visit Round Trees Garden Centre tearoom, TL and continue for 1km/0.6 mile. Otherwise, TR at TJ, SP Clevedon/Kenn (16.5km/10.5 miles). Continue through Yatton, passing station on LHS. Shortly afterwards:

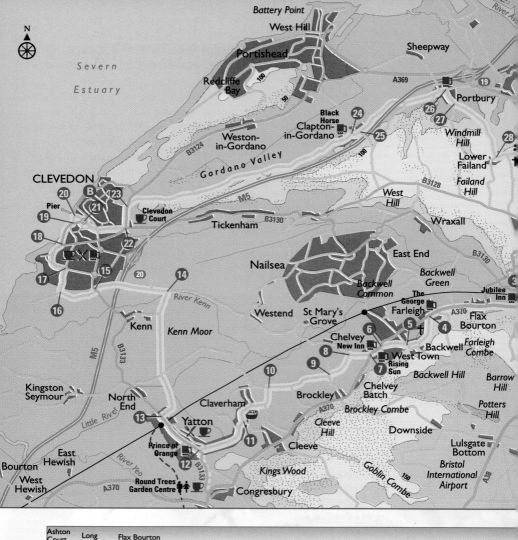

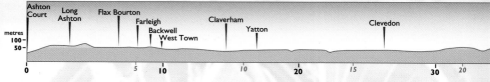

13 TR along Kenn Moor Road, no SP, through housing estate and onto flat, straight road.

14 TL at TJ next to Rosecroft Cottage, no SP. **22.5km (14 miles)**

15 TL at TJ for 100m, no SP but SP to motorway if TR (25km/15.5 miles). TR, no SP, cross old railway bridge and pass Colehouse Caravan Park on RHS.

16 TR at TJ along Strode Road, no SP.

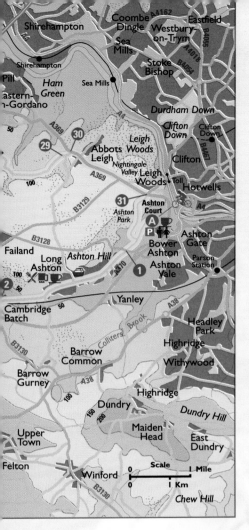

19 TL along The Beach, no SP (next to telephone box on LHS). Descend towards pier. Just before pier entrance:

20 TR, SP Hill Road. Climb.

21 SO at large roundabout along Linden Road, no SP (29km/18 miles). TL along Princes Road. At end of road, TR at XR for 40m, no SP. Then TL (opposite church) along Highdale Road. Descend.

22 TL at TJ along Old Street, no SP. Immediately TL at mini roundabout, SP Portishead.

23 TR along Wortons Wood Lane, SP Clapton-in-Gordano. ***31km (19 miles)***

24 TR at TJ, SP Portbury. Climb.

25 TL (effectively SO) along Caswell Lane, no SP.

26 TR at TJ along High Street, SP Portishead/Bristol (41km/25.5 miles). TR at mini roundabout along Mill Lane, SP Failand/Bristol.

27 TL along Failand Lane, no SP. Climb (this lane is especially beautiful in spring when it is full of bluebells).

28 TL at TJ along Sandy Lane, no SP.

29 RHF along Harris Lane, SP Clifton/Bristol.

30 TR at TJ onto A369 and climb, no SP (47.5km/29.5 miles). Pass George Inn on RHS and arrive traffic lights – road forks in two directions (at traffic lights) to Bristol and Clifton. Dismount to:

31 TR, no SP. Pass through gatehouse into Ashton Court. Continue through barrier and along this road for fast descent to the end of the ride. ***51.5km (32 miles)***

If you started from Yatton station, continue to visitor centre and follow route directions from start.

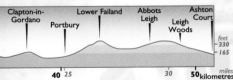

17 TL at TJ, no SP. Pass Strode Leisure Centre on RHS.

18 TL at TJ along Elton Road, SP Sea Front. Continue along sea front.

MARLBOROUGH AND THE KENNET AND AVON CANAL

Route information

Distance   52.5km (32.5 miles)

Grade   Easy

Terrain   A steep climb at the start but the route soon flattens out along the canal and the River Kennet valley.

Time to allow   3–6 hours.

Getting there by car   Marlborough is on the east side of Wiltshire. Leave the M4 at junction 15 and take the A345 into Marlborough. There is long-term pay and display parking next to the Tourist Information Centre – follow SP from the High Street.

Getting there by train   There is no railway station at Marlborough. However both Great Bedwyn and Hungerford have stations. From Great Bedwyn station TR and continue SO at direction 11, SP Marlborough/Little Bedwyn. From Hungerford, TR out of station, TR onto A338. Continue route at direction 14.

From Marlborough the route heads south to Wootton Rivers. The route then follows the Kennet and Avon Canal as it passes through the villages of Great and Little Bedwyn before arriving in Hungerford. The route returns to Marlborough following the River Kennet, as it meanders through the pretty villages of Ramsbury, Axford and Mildenhall.

Places of interest along the route

Ⓐ Marlborough

King Arthur's magician Merlin is reputedly buried here under a mound, so giving Marlborough its original name of Merle Barrow. See route 12 for further details.

Ⓑ Crofton Beam Engines, Crofton

Two 19th-century steam engines, one built in 1812 and the oldest working beam engine in the world, the other built in 1845. They are steamed Easter–August on some weekends. The pumping station and engines are open for viewing Easter–October, daily 1030–1700. Café. Charge. Telephone (01672) 870300 for further information.

Ⓒ Great Bedwyn Stone Museum, Great Bedwyn

The work of seven generations of the Lloyd family, who originally arrived here to work on the Kennet and Avon Canal, is on display at the museum. The house and yard are littered with ornamental masonry, fossils and amusing epitaphs. Open Monday–Friday, during normal trading hours, although carrying home a souvenir could prove a little tricky. Admission free. Telephone (01672) 870234.

Ⓓ Kennet and Avon Canal

Authorized by parliament in 1794 and opened in 1810, the Kennet and Avon runs for 139km (87 miles) between Bristol and Reading. It declined more slowly than other canals in the country, eventually closing in 1955. However in 1958 the Kennet and Avon Trust was set up and the entire canal was re-opened in 1990. It now provides a beautiful green corridor along which you can boat, cycle and walk. Note you must have a permit to cycle along the Kennet and Avon Canal. See page 8 for details.

Food and drink

Lots of places in Marlborough and Hungerford. Burbage has a pub, convenience store and garage, and there are pubs and stores in Great Bedwyn and Ramsbury. Refreshments are also available at Crofton Beam Engines.

Royal Oak, Wootton Rivers
Thatched pub with attractive outside seating in a courtyard. Open all day.

Tutti-Pole Teashoppe, Hungerford
Friendly family-run teashop.

Wheatsheaf, Chilton Foliat
Thatched pub offering meals.

Red Lion Inn, Axford
Egon Ronay listed, specializing in seafood and fish.

Horseshoe Inn, Mildenhall
Another thatched pub. Outdoor seating.

Route description

Start from the Tourist Information Centre at Marlborough. Follow exit road round to left to TR at TJ, SP Chippenham/Calne/Pewsey.

1 TL at TJ onto A345, SP Amesbury/Salisbury/Pewsey/Upavon. Continue on A345 to climb Granham Hill.

2 TL (effectively SO), SP Clench Common/Wootton Rivers. The road gently climbs to lovely viewpoint, followed by fast descent.

3 TL, SP Wootton Rivers.

4 TL at TJ for 200m, no SP (8km/5 miles). Then TR at TJ, SP Easton Royal/Milton Lilbourne. Continue through Wootton Rivers to cross Kennet and Avon Canal.

5 TR at TJ, SP Easton Royal. Enter village.

6 TL at TJ, SP Burbage.

7 TL at large roundabout (second exit) along High Street, SP Burbage.

8 TR along Taskers Lane, no SP.

15km (9.5 miles)

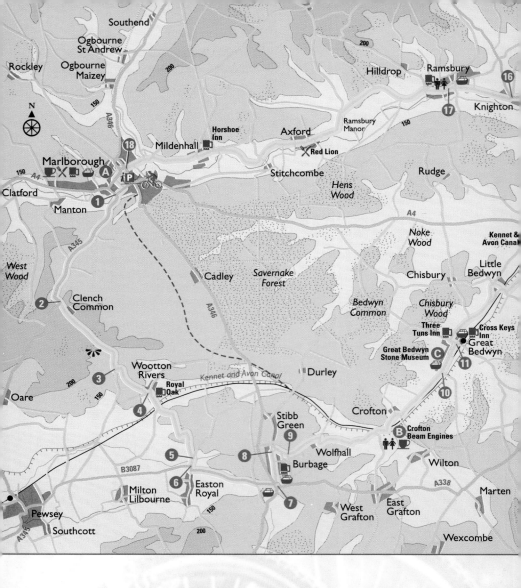

Southend

Ogbourne
St Andrew

Rockley

Ogbourne
Maizey

200

150

A346

18

Mildenhall

Horshoe
Inn

Axford

Ramsbury
Manor

Hilldrop

Ramsbury

Knighton

16

17

150

Red Lion

Stitchcombe

Rudge

Marlborough

150

A4

A

P

Clatford

Manton

1

Hens
Wood

A4

Noke
Wood

Kennet &
Avon Canal

A345

West
Wood

2

Clench
Common

Cadley

A346

Savernake
Forest

Bedwyn
Common

Chisbury
Wood

Chisbury

Little
Bedwyn

Three
Tuns Inn

Cross Keys
Inn

Great Bedwyn
Stone Museum

C

Great
Bedwyn

3

200

150

Wootton
Rivers

Royal
Oak

Kennet and Avon Canal

Durley

11

10

Oare

4

Stibb
Green

9

Crofton

B

Crofton
Beam Engines

Wolfhall

5

B3087

8

Burbage

Wilton

6

Milton
Lilbourne

Easton
Royal

7

A338

Marten

150

West
Grafton

East
Grafton

Pewsey

200

Southcott

Wexcombe

A345

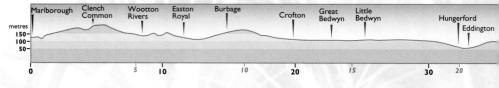

	Marlborough	Clench Common	Wootton Rivers	Easton Royal	Burbage	Crofton	Great Bedwyn	Little Bedwyn	Hungerford	Eddington

metres
150—
100—
50—

0   5   10   10   20   15   30   20

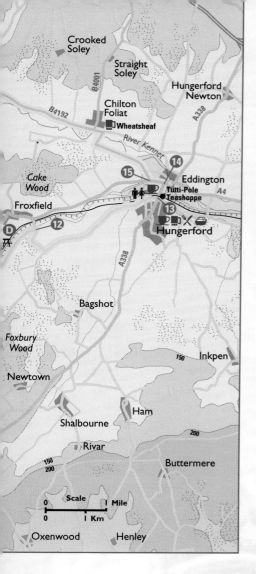

9 TL, SP Wolfhall/Crofton. Follow this quiet lane towards windmill. Continue through Crofton, passing Crofton Beam Engines on RHS.

10 TL (effectively SO) at TJ, SP Bedwyn. Enter Great Bedwyn and pass Great Bedwyn Stone Museum on LHS.

11 TL at TJ, SP Marlborough/Little Bedwyn. Pass Cross Keys Inn then convenience store on RHS. TR along Browns Lane, SP Hungerford/Little Bedwyn/Froxfield (in front of Three Tuns Inn). Continue along this road into Little Bedwyn. Cross railway and follow canal close to its edge (good picnic sites).

12 TR, SP North Standen (27km/17 miles). Climb gently then descend into Hungerford.

13 TL at mini roundabout, no SP. Pass under bridge and cross canal.

14 TL at mini roundabout, SP Marlborough/Swindon. **32km (20 miles)**

15 TR, SP Aldbourne/Ramsbury/Chilton Foliat.

16 TL at XR, SP Ramsbury/Marlborough. Enter Ramsbury and in centre of village:

17 TL at TJ and descend High Street, no SP (41km/25.5 miles). Leave village to climb around Ramsbury Manor. Continue through Axford and Mildenhall towards Marlborough.

18 SO at XR opposite small green, no SP. TL at TJ to return to centre of Marlborough or, TR at TJ (opposite Ailesbury Court) to TL down Hilliers Yard (just past Waitrose) to complete the ride. **52.5km (32.5 miles)**

If you started from Great Bedwyn or Hungerford, follow directions from start of route.

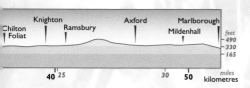

ILCHESTER TO CASTLE CARY

Route information

Distance 52km (32.5 miles)

Grade Moderate

Terrain On-road throughout. The south east section of the route is hilly; the north and west are flat.

Time to allow 4–6 hours.

Getting there by car Ilchester is just off the A303, on the A37/B3151. There is a free long-stay car park at the south end of town.

Getting there by train There is no railway station at Ilchester. However, there is a station at Castle Cary. Exit the station to TL for approximately 0.5km (0.3 mile), TR, SP Castle Cary, and join the route at direction 16 where TR.

From Ilchester the route heads east along quiet roads to Sandford Orcas. From here you head north to Castle Cary, passing the romantic Cadbury Castle. The route now heads south west along undulating roads back to Ilchester.

Places of interest along the route

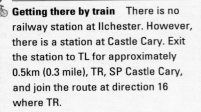

Ⓐ Ilchester

Once the principal Roman settlements in Somerset, Ilchester was the county town until the mid-19th century. Today there is little to suggest this bar a few 18th-century buildings.

The town's history can be explored in the **Ilchester Museum** which concentrates particularly on the Roman period. Open Easter to September, Thursday and Saturday 1000–1600. Admission free. Telephone (01935) 841247.

Ⓑ Cadbury Castle, South Cadbury

Reached via a steep track to the south of South Cadbury, Cadbury Castle is reputed to be King Arthur's mythical fortress, from which a causeway stretched to Glastonbury. In reality, it is a marvellous hill top plateau with added fortifications. Occupied since 3300 BC, it has been used by generations of people. The views of the surrounding area are great and are well worth the diversion. Admission free. Open at all reasonable times.

Ⓒ Castle Cary

One of the prettiest towns in Somerset. The town's history is laid out in the small **museum** sited above the attractive arched Market Hall. Open April to October, Monday–Saturday 1000–1200 and 1430–1630. Admission free. Telephone (01963) 50277. Do not miss the tiny **Round House** lock up which was built in 1779 and is one of only four surviving in the country.

Ⓓ Fleet Air Arm Museum, Ilchester

The museum depicts the history of the Fleet Air Arm, the navy's airforce. Over 40 aircraft from World War I to the present day are on display, including Concorde 002. There are audio-visual displays of life on a 1970s aircraft carrier, as well as photographs and memorabilia. Gift shop. Café/restaurant (admission free). Open daily, summer 1000–1730; winter 1000–1630. Charge. Telephone (01935) 840565.

Food and drink

Plenty of choice in Ilchester and Castle Cary. There is a pub in Corton Denham. Refreshments are also available at the Fleet Air Arm Museum.

Lamb and Lark, Limington
Tea and coffee, bar snacks and meals offered here.

 Catash Inn, North Cadbury
Offers bar and restaurant meals.

Red Lion Inn, Babcary
Pub meals and outside seating.

 Walnut Tree, West Camel
Egon Ronay listed restaurant. Also hotel and stores.

Cadbury Castle

Route description

Start from Ilchester Town Hall/Community Centre to TR along Church Street, passing Ilchester Arms then church on LHS. Just before free car park/toilets:

1 TL, SP Limington/Mudford. Continue on this road, through Limington.

2 TL, SP Mudford.

3 TL at TJ, SP Marston Magna/Sparkford. Cross River Yeo.

4 TR, SP Adber/Trent. Start to climb.
8km (5 miles)

5 SO at staggered XR across B3148, SP Sandford Orcas. Continue for steep descent into Sandford Orcas.

6 TL to visit Sandford Orcas Manor. Otherwise, TR at TJ, SP Sherbourne. Then TL, SP Holway/Corton Denham/Poyntington. Continue on this road through Corton Denham.

7 TR, SP South Cadbury/Compton Pauncefoot (16.5km/10.5 miles). Views of Cadbury Castle straight ahead.

8 TR at TJ, SP South Cadbury. Pass Red Lion pub then entrance to Cadbury Castle on LHS. Cross A303 and continue into North Cadbury. Pass Catash Inn on RHS and as road bears left:

9 TR, SP Galhampton.

10 TL at TJ, no SP (22.5km/14 miles). Then TR along March Lane, no SP.

11 TR opposite Chapel Farm, no SP. Pass village hall on RHS.

12 TL along Frog Lane, no SP. Pass picnic spot (seat) with views of Cadbury Castle.

13 SO at XR along Small Way Lane, SP Castle Cary.

14 TR at TJ, no SP. Enter Castle Cary.

15 TL at TJ, no SP (by Lower Woodcock Street).

16 TL, SP North Barrow/Lovington/ Somerton. Continue along Torbay Road.

17 TR at TJ, no SP (33km/20.5 miles). Continue through North Barrow.

18 SO at XR, SP Babcary.

19 TL at TJ, SP Babcary/Charlton Mackrell.

20 TR at TJ, SP Babcary/Charlton Mackrell.

21 TL (effectively SO) along narrower lane next to Red Lion (39.5km/24.5 miles), no SP (other road bears right, SP Charlton Mackrell/Keinton Mandeville). Pass Red Lion Inn then Wessex Water Babcary Orchard Cottage Pumping Station for hard climb.

22 SO across A303 at XR WITH CARE, SP West Camel. Descend Howell Hill.

23 TR at XR, SP Bridgehampton/Ilchester.

24 TL at XR, no SP (48km/30 miles). Keep airbase on LHS and pass entrance to Fleet Air Arm Museum. Enter Ilchester.

25 TL at large roundabout, no SP and continue back to Town Hall/Community Centre to complete the ride. *52m (32.5 miles)*

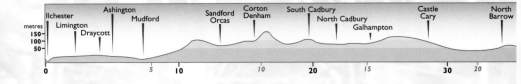

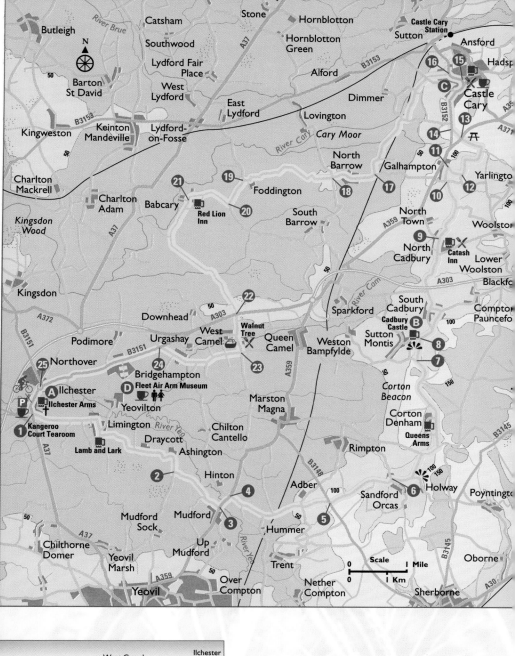

Butleigh
Catsham
Stone
Hornblotton
Castle Cary Station
Sutton
Ansford
Hadsp
16
15
Southwood
Hornblotton Green
C
Lydford Fair Place
Alford
Castle Cary
13
West Lydford
Dimmer
14
11
Barton St David
East Lydford
Lovington
North Barrow
Galhampton
Yarlingto
Kingweston
Keinton Mandeville
Lydford-on-Fosse
Cary Moor
17
12
10
Charlton Mackrell
19
Foddington
18
North Town
Woolstor
Charlton Adam
Babcary
21
20
South Barrow
9
North Cadbury
Catash Inn
Lower Woolston
Kingsdon Wood
Red Lion Inn
Blackfc
Kingsdon
22
Downhead
Sparkford
South Cadbury
Compto Pauncefo
Podimore
West Camel
Walnut Tree
Queen Camel
Cadbury Castle
B
Northover
Urgashay
Weston Bampfylde
Sutton Montis
8
25
Ilchester
Bridgehampton
Fleet Air Arm Museum
23
7
A
Ilchester Arms
Yeovilton
Marston Magna
Corton Beacon
Kangeroo Court Tearoom
Limington
Chilton Cantello
Corton Denham
1
Draycott
Ashington
Rimpton
Queens Arms
Lamb and Lark
2
Hinton
4
Adber
6
Holway
Poynto
Mudford Sock
Mudford
3
Sandford Orcas
5
Chilthorne Domer
Up Mudford
Hummer
Oborne
Yeovil Marsh
Trent
Nether Compton
Sherborne
Yeovil
Over Compton

Scale
0 — 1 Mile
0 — 1 Km

Foddington
Babcary
West Camel
Bridgehampton
Northover
Ilchester
feet
490
330
165
40 25
30
50
miles
kilometres

TAUNTON AND BRIDGWATER

Route information

Distance   57km (35.5 miles)

Grade   Easy

Terrain   A long section of canal towpath, suitable for most bicycles, and quiet, mostly flat roads and lanes.

Time to allow   4–8 hours.

Getting there by car   Taunton is just north of junction 25 off the M5. The best place to park is at the free canalside car park close to the cattle market.

Getting there by train   There is a railway station at Taunton. Telephone (0345) 484950 for travel information.

Starting at Taunton station the ride utilises the entire length of the recently restored towpath of the Bridgwater & Taunton Canal. At Bridgwater you return a short way along the canal before following the Rivers Parrett and Tone. A series of quiet roads through pretty villages leads back to the canal at Creech St Michael for the return to Taunton.

Places of interest along the route

A Taunton

The county town of Somerset, Taunton prides itself on its parks and gardens, winning regional awards in the Britain in Bloom competitions. It also boasts one of the finest church towers in the country, on St Mary Magdalene church.

The **Somerset County Museum**, incorporating the Museum of the Somerset Light Infantry, is located in the castle and displays interesting finds from around Somerset. Open April to October, Tuesday–Saturday and Bank Holiday Mondays 1000–1700; November to March, Tuesday–Saturday 1000–1500. Charge. Telephone (01823) 320201.Taunton is the home of Somerset Cricket Club and its history is displayed in the **Somerset Cricket Museum** at the county ground. Open April to November, Monday–Friday 1000–1600. Nominal charge. Telephone (01823) 275893. There is much else to see in Taunton. Telephone the Tourist Information Centre for more details (see page 13).

B Bridgwater and Taunton Canal

Opened in 1827, the Bridgwater and Taunton Canal provides a link between the two towns. In 1994 a 23-km (14.5-mile) length was reopened following lengthy restoration. Note: you must have a permit to cycle along the canal. See page 8 for details. Something totally unique has been placed alongside the canal – the **Somerset Space Walk** is an attempt to quantify the true size of the solar system. Small scale models of the planets are placed along the towpath in true proportion to their distance and size. The effect is an appreciation of the true magnitude of the solar system. Unfortunately for cyclists most planets are on a section that cannot be cycled, but do not miss Pluto at either end of the canal. Mid way along the

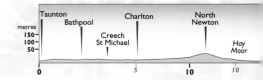

canal, in the only remaining lock cottage, is **Maunsel Canal Centre**, which describes the canal and its history. Tea garden. Open all year, Monday–Friday in the afternoon; weekends and Bank Holidays, all day. Admission free. Telephone (01278) 663160.

ⓒ Bridgwater

Formerly a busy port until overshadowed by Bristol, today Bridgwater is an industrial centre, noted for its magnificent annual carnival. Held on the Thursday closest to Guy Fawkes night, the carnival features many illuminated floats on varying themes. Robert Blake, one of Cromwell's admirals, was born in the town and his former home houses the **Admiral Blake Museum**. Featuring the local history of Bridgwater, the museum includes a description of the Battle of Sedgemoor. Open all year, Tuesday–Saturday 1000–1600. Admission free. Telephone (01278) 456127.

ⓓ Westonzoyland Pumping Station, Moorland

Volunteers have restored the 1861 Easton and Amos drainage machine that helped prevent flooding of the Somerset Levels. Also a small forge, works tramway and other steam exhibits. Open all year, Sunday 1400–1700; also Bank Holiday Mondays and June to August, Thursday 1400–2000. Charge. Telephone (01823) 275795.

ⓔ St Michael's, Barrow Mump

The ruins of St Michael's can be seen for miles around. In use until at least 1633, this was the site of a stand by Royalist troops after the Battle of Langport. A failed appeal for rebuilding in 1793 leaves the ruins as seen today. National Trust property. Free access at all reasonable times.

ⓕ Willows and Wetlands Visitor Centre, Stoke St Gregory

The Coate family have been creating baskets from local withies since 1819. The visitor centre explains the basket-making process. Also exhibition and video on the wetlands. Open all year, daily 0900–1700. Admission free. Guided tour Monday–Friday, every half hour (charge). Telephone (01823) 490249.

Route description

Starting from Taunton railway station, follow SP exit. TL at TJ to follow one-way system, no SP. Then LHF, SP Railway Station/Market/Town Centre and pass under railway bridge.

1 TL at traffic lights, no SP. Immediately TL along Canal Road, no SP (opposite Market Hall/Produce Market). Pass toilets, market and canalside parking on RHS.

2 RHF, SP National Cycleway 3. Pass through gates onto towpath. Cross canal next to lock and continue along towpath.

3 TR, no SP but opposite where towpath deteriorates to grass (11km/7 miles), to TL at TJ along tarmac, no SP. Cross canal next to Sun (part of Somerset Space Walk). Continue into North Newton, following SP North Newton.

4 TR at TJ, SP North Petherton/Bridgwater (14.5km/9 miles). Then TR along Church Road, SP NC3. Pass Harvest Moon pub, bear right in front of church, cross canal and bear left following tarmac towpath. Pass Boat and Anchor pub and:

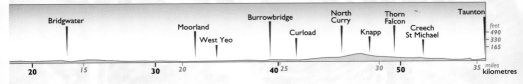

5   TL, no SP. Cross canal to TR, SP National Cyclway 3. Continue on tarmac with canal on right. When road bears left:

6   TR back onto canal towpath. Follow towpath into Bridgwater. When canal widens to accommodate boating moorings, follow towpath to road and TL at TJ for 20m, no SP. Then TR to pass behind other widening and cross narrow bridge over canal as it drains into River Parrett. Bear left along path, keeping River Parrett close on LHS. Cross small then larger roads and continue SO, SP Citizens Advice Bureau. Pass main pedestrianised street on RHS. Then bear right in front of library along Chapel Street, SP National Cycleway 3.

7   TL at XR opposite Frian Street, SP Barnstaple/Taunton/Exeter.

26.5km (16.5 miles)

8   SO at XR (traffic lights), SP Huntworth/ North Petherton. Cross A39 (dual carriageway). At SP canal:

9   TR opposite Elmwood Avenue, no SP. Descend onto towpath and TR sharply along towpath, to pass under road.

10   TL, cross canal and bear right, passing Boat and Anchor Inn on LHS. At the next bridge:

11   TL, no SP (29.5km/18.5 miles). Climb slope to leave towpath and TL at TJ, no SP. Cross weak bridge and enter Moorland. Pass Thatchers Arms pub and Westonzoyland Pumping Station. Continue, following SP Burrowbridge.

12   SO at XR, SP Oath.

13   TR along Stanmoor Road, SP Athelney/ Stoke St Gregory/North Curry. Enter Stoke St Gregory and cross railway.

14   TR at TJ, SP North Curry/Taunton/ Willows and Wetlands (41.5km/26 miles). Pass Willows and Wetlands Visitor Centre on RHS. Continue into North Curry.

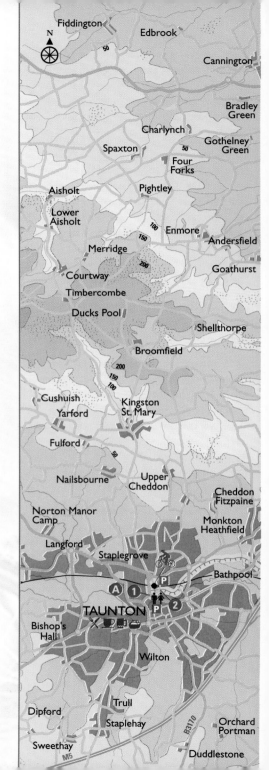

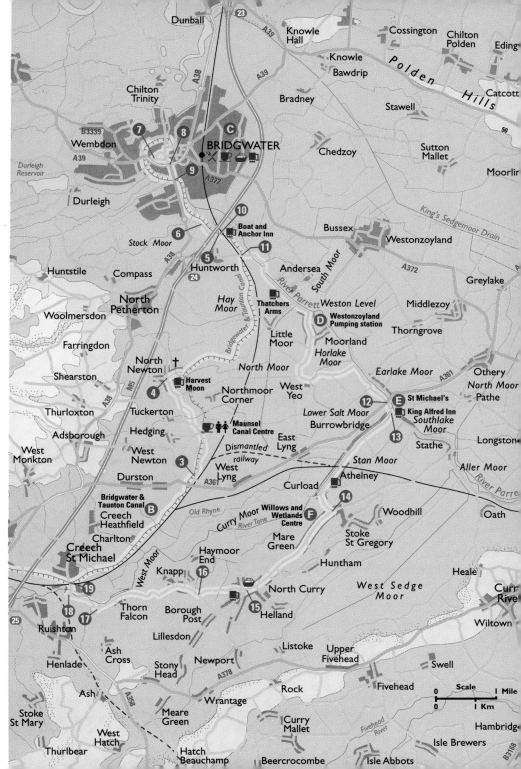

The River Parrett at Burrow Bridge

15 TR next to stone memorial, no SP. Bear left then SO at XR along Knapp Lane, SP Knapp/Creech St Michael. Pass White Hart Inn.

16 TR at TJ, SP Knapp/Creech.

17 TR at TJ, SP Creech St Michael/ Taunton. **49.5km (31 miles)**

18 TR at TJ, SP Creech St Michael/Bridgewater. Cross river. Enter Creech St Michael and bear left. Cross railway and:

19 TR onto canal, no SP. Once on towpath, TL to pass under road. Follow towpath into Taunton. When towpath crosses canal (next to locks), TR (effectively SO) through gates and onto road. Pass cattle market LHS. TR at TJ, no SP. Then TR at TJ, SP Station and complete the ride. **57km (35.5 miles)**

Food and drink

Lots of choice in Taunton and Bridgewater. North Curry has pubs and convenience stores. The Pigeons in Stoke St Gregory is closed Monday and Tuesday. Refreshments are also available at the Maunsel Canal Centre.

Harvest Moon, North Newton
Pub meals available.

Boat and Anchor Inn, near Huntworth
Food served all day.

Thatchers Arms, Moorland
Home cooked food offered.

King Alfred Inn, Burrow Bridge
Open daily (all day on Sundays).

Route
19 EXMOOR – DUNSTER TO PORLOCK

Route information

Distance 70.5km (44 miles)

Grade Strenuous

Terrain On-road throughout, with both long steady and short steep climbs. There is a long section of A road at the end of the route.

Time to allow 5–9 hours.

Getting there by car Dunster is on the A39 Minehead to Bridgwater road. There is a long-term car park (pay and display) as you enter the village on the A39.

Getting there by train There is a railway station at Dunster. Telephone (0345) 484950 for information.

From the lovely village of Dunster the route follows the River Avill valley to Timberscombe. From here a long steady climb over the Brendon Hills leads to a pleasant descent to the attractive town of Dulverton. Another long steady climb takes you across Exmoor, the effort amply compensated for by the views. On through Exford and across the moor before a steep descent into Porlock. The route follows the A39 through the seaside resort of Minehead back to Dunster.

Route description

Start from Dunster Station. TL at TJ for 400m, no SP. TL at TJ, no SP, and cycle through village, passing Conygar View on LHS.

1 TL onto cyclepath just before A39, no SP. TR, SP Subway/Dunster/Carhampton, and pass under A39 to TL sharply, SP Dunster.

Exmoor

2 TR at TJ, no SP (1km/0.6 mile). Climb through Dunster. Pass Exmoor Visitor Centre on LHS. Continue to Timberscombe.

3 TL, SP Timberscombe.

4 TL, SP Luxborough/Brompton Regis (6.5km/4 miles). Climb for further 6.5km (4 miles).

5 SO at XR (Heath Poult Cross), SP Brompton Regis/Dulverton. Descend.

6 TR at TJ, SP Dulverton/Minehead.
23km (14.5 miles)

7 TL, SP Dulverton, and continue into Dulverton.

8 TR along Union Street, SP Library/Visitor Centre (25.5km/16 miles). Then SO at XR along Lady Street, SP Lynton/Exford/Tarr Steps. Continue on this road towards Exford.

9 TR at XR, SP Exford/Minehead. Descend.
41km (25.5 miles)

10 TR at TJ, SP Wheddon Cross/ Taunton/ Minehead. Cross bridge.

11 TL along Pork Street, SP Cloutsham/ Porlock (42.5km/26.5 miles). Follow river on left, then climb through woods to reaching open moorland and far reaching views.

12 To visit Porlock Weir, TL at TJ for approximately 3km (2 miles), SP Lynton. Take second TR along Toll Road into Porlock. At foot of hill follow road past Porlock Weir and into Porlock. TL at TJ onto A39 in Porlock and continue along A39 to direction 13.

Otherwise, TR at TJ, SP Porlock/Minehead. Steeply descend Porlock Hill WITH CARE into Porlock.

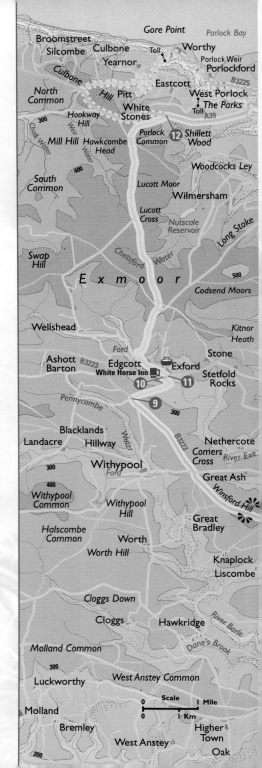

13 TL, SP Minehead (64km/40 miles). Follow road through centre of Minehead.

14 TL at large roundabout, SP Bridgwater/Taunton.

15 SO at roundabout, SP Willaton/Taunton/Bridgewater.

16 TL, SP Marsh Street/Dunster Station.

17 TL, SP Dunster Station/Dunster Beach.

18 TR into the station, no SP, and complete the ride.   ***70.5km (44 miles)***

Food and drink

Dunster, Porlock and Minehead have a wide selection of places for refreshment. There is a post office/stores in Timberscombe, tearooms at Dulverton and convenience stores at Exford. Refreshments are also available at Dunster Water Mill.

Lion Inn, Timberscombe
Food available at lunchtime (except Monday).

White Horse Inn, Exford
Pub with tearoom.

Places of interest along the route

A Dunster
Once renowned for it's woollen industry, Dunster is one of the prettiest villages in the country. There has been a **castle** here since Norman times. Standing on top of a wooded hill, the castle was the home of the Luttrell family for 600 years. The 13th-century gatehouse survives, but the present building was remodelled between 1868 and 1872. There are pleasant walks in the surrounding parkland. Picnic area. National Trust property. Castle open April to October, Saturday–Wednesday 1100–1700. Garden and park open all year, daily 1000–1600. Charge. Telephone (01643) 821314. Close to the castle is **Dunster Water Mill**, mentioned in the Domesday Book and grinding corn until 1962. The present mill was restored to working order in 1979. Tearoom and garden. National Trust property. Open April to October, daily 1030–1700 (closed Saturdays April–June, September and October). Charge. Telephone (01643) 821759. The **Doll Museum** features an immense variety of dolls of all ages. Open April to October, Sunday–Friday 1030– 1700. Charge. Telephone (01643) 821220. More information on the surrounding area can be obtained from the Exmoor Visitor Centre at the north end of the village, telephone (01643) 821835.

B Porlock
Occupying a lovely site between the sea and Exmoor, Porlock, mentioned *Lorna Doone*, is well worth exploring. A 15th-century building contains the Tourist Information Centre and the

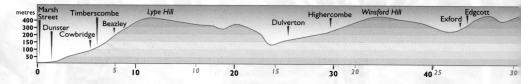

Porlock Bay from Exmoor

Porlock Museum, which describes local history. Open all year, Monday–Friday 1000–1300 and 1400–1700, Saturday 1000–1300 and 1430–1630. Admission free. If time permits, a trip to the lovely Porlock Weir, the site of Porlock's 19th-century harbour, is recommended.

C Minehead

Until the 18th century Minehead derived it's wealth from the port and associated herring fleets. Unfortunately the herrings disappeared and the harbour silted up. However, the arrival of the West Somerset railway in 1854 and the ensuing Victorian enjoyment of seaside holidays led to its establishment as a holiday resort. The influx of tourists continues to this day. As a result there are all the usual seaside trappings from amusement arcades and fish and chips to a seaside promenade.

Route information

- **Distance**   74.5km (46.5 miles)

- **Grade**   Moderate

- **Terrain**   Undulating roads to the south; the northern section of the route is over the flat Somerset Levels.

- **Time to allow**   5–9 hours.

- **Getting there by car**   Somerton is in south Somerset on the B3153 east of Langport. There is a long-stay car park next to the Half Moon pub, just west of the Tourist Information Centre and the library.

- **Getting there by train**   Although the railway runs through Somerton, there is no station and therefore no practical rail access to this route.

From the attractive country town of Somerton, the route heads west towards Low Ham. A steep climb takes you past England's only thatched windmill before a descent towards the Polden Hills. A pleasant traverse through a series of attractive villages brings you to Woolavington for a descent to the Somerset Levels. The route now heads east towards Glastonbury before turning south and returning to Somerton.

Places of interest along the route

A Stembridge Tower Mill, near Somerton
Dating from 1822, Stembridge Tower Mill is the last thatched windmill in England. National Trust property. Open Easter to September, Sunday, Monday and Wednesday 1400–1700. Charge. Telephone (01458) 250818.

B Coombes Cider Farm, near Mark
An opportunity for cider sampling. Also children's play area, video describing the cider maker's year and adjacent Apple Blossom Tearooms. Open Mon-Sat 0900-1830. Admission free.

C Peat Moors Visitor Centre, near Westhay
Celebrating the life, archaeology and history of the Somerset Levels and Moors, the visitor centre features the Avalon Marshes. Reconstructions of trackways and housing demonstrate how man has lived and worked in this area. Open March, weekends 1000–1700; April to October, daily 1000–1700 every day. Charge. Telephone (01458) 860697. Tearoom in adjacent Willows Garden Centre.

D Glastonbury
A potent mix of Christianity and Arthurian legend are on hand in the lovely town of Glastonbury. See route 10 for further details.

Food and drink

Plenty of choice in Somerton and Glastonbury, and a village store in Chilton Poldon. In addition to those featured below, the following serve food: King William Inn, Catcott; White Hart, Edington; Prince of Wales, Woolavington; The Crown, East Huntspill; Basonbridge Inn, Bason Bridge. Refreshments are also available close to Coombes Cider Farm and Peat Moor Visitor Centre.

Albion Inn, Ashcott
Serves an all day breakfast.

Red Tile, Cossington
Free house serving food.

Watchfield Inn, Watchfield
Real ale and pub meals. Also garden, camping and caravan park.

Ye Olde Burtle Inn, Burtle
Food served all day on Sunday. Also outside seating and campsite.

Rose and Portcullis, Butleigh
Bar and restaurant meals. Garden.

Route description

Start from the square in the centre of Somerton (by White Hart Inn, St Michaels and All Angels Church and war memorial). TR along West Street, SP Toilets. Pass Tourist Information Centre, short-stay car park, Half Moon pub and long-stay car park on RHS.

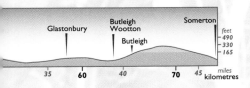

1 RHF, SP B3153/Langport.

2 TL (effectively SO) at mini roundabout, SP Langport. Pass Catholic Church on RHS.

3 TR, SP Westcombe/Low Ham. Continue on this road.

4 TR, SP Low Ham.

5 SO at XR, no SP. Climb quite steeply. Pass Stembridge Tower Mill on LHS.

6 TR at XR, no SP. Pass Forth House on LHS.

7 TR at TJ opposite church, no SP. Continue on this road. **8km (5 miles)**

8 TR at TJ along A361, SP Street/Glastonbury. Then TL, no SP, for climb, passing Pedwell Methodist Church on LHS.

9 TL at TJ, SP Bridgwater. Then TR along Shapwick Hill, SP Shapwick/Westhay.

10 TL, no SP (16km/10 miles). Pass between 30mph SP. Follow this road through Catcott, Edington and Chilton Polden.

11 TR along Manor Road, SP Woolavington. Then bear left, SP Woolavington/Bason Bridge.

12 TR at XR, SP Woolavington/East Huntspill. Continue through East Huntspill and Bason Bridge.

13 TR at TJ, SP Wedmore/Wells. Continue into Mark. Pass Coombes Cider Farm on LHS.

14 TR at XR along Yardwall Road, SP Burtle/Edington/Glastonbury.

15 TR at TJ, SP Edington/Glastonbury (37.5km/23.5 miles). Continue through Burtle.

16 TR at TJ, SP Shapwick/Bridgwater. Pass Peat Moors Visitor Centre on LHS. Continue into Shapwick.

17 TL at TJ along Northbrook Road, SP NC3.

18 TR, SP NC3 (49.5km/31 miles). View of Glastonbury Tor straight ahead.

19 TL at TJ, SP NC3. Pass postbox on LHS. Then TR along Whitley Lane, SP NC3.

20 TL, SP NC3.

21 TL at TJ, SP NC3. Pass Wet Park Farm on RHS. Follow road as it bears right next to peat heaps.

22 TL at TJ, SP NC3.   **56km (35 miles)**

23 TR at TJ, SP Glastonbury/Street.

24 TL, no SP. Cross weak bridge.

25 SO at mini roundabout, past SP Dead End. Cross A39 and pass through gap in wall, SP Glastonbury Town Centre. Pass Scout/Guide HQ on RHS. Pass to left of church.

26 TR at TJ, SP Wearyall Mill/Rural Life Museum/Toilets. Pass town hall on LHS.

27 TL (effectively SO) at mini roundabout, SP Frome/S Mallet. Short climb.

28 TR (effectively SO) along Butleigh Road, SP Butleigh. Leave Glastonbury and continue towards Butleigh Wootton.

29 TL at TJ, SP Butleigh (63.5km/39.5 miles). Continue through Butleigh Wootton to Butleigh.

30 TL at TJ, SP Kingweston/Somerton.

31 TR at TJ, SP Somerton/Langport. Descend central lined road towards Somerton.

32 TL at TJ onto B3153, SP Somerton/Langport/Ilchester/Yeovil (74km/46 miles). Continue towards Somerton.

33 TR along B3153, SP Somerton. Climb into town.

34 TL at mini roundabout along North Street, no SP. Continue into square to finish the ride.   **74.5km (46.5 miles)**

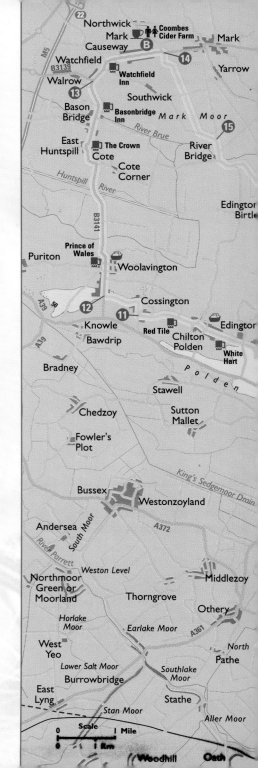

Route information

Distance   78km (48.5 miles)

Grade   Moderate

Terrain   There are two long sections of track that although mostly firm should not be tackled on a road bike. However, they are of mild gradient and are not technically challenging. The on-road cycling follows mostly quiet lanes, with one long climb.

Time to allow   6–9 hours.

Getting there by car   Salisbury is in south Wiltshire on the A36. There are many places to park, including a pay and display car park at the railway station.

Getting there by train   There is a railway station at Salisbury. Telephone (0345) 484950 for travel information.

Starting from the beautiful cathedral city of Salisbury, the route heads west out of the city and along an ancient sheep drover's track. As is usual for byways close to towns, the start is a little rough and rubbish strewn but the track soon opens out to pass through woodland and fields with lovely views to either side. A steep descent and a short section of A road lead to the attractive town of Shaftesbury, where the prime attraction is Gold Hill, made famous by the Hovis adverts. The route back to Salisbury follows an oxen track, again with magnificent views, and then quiet roads through the pleasant villages of Bowerchalke and Bishopstone.

Places of interest along the route

A Salisbury

Salisbury has retained much of its architectural heritage and it is well worth taking the time to explore the town. It is dominated by the spire of **Salisbury Cathedral**. Built in 1220 and completed 38 years later, the cathedral is home to Britain's oldest clock which still strikes on the hour. Close to the cathedral is **Mompesson House**. Owned by the National Trust, this is a small Queen Anne town house once home of the Bishop. Inside there is magnificent plasterwork, an intricate oak staircase and a fine collection of 18th-century drinking glasses. Open April to October, Saturday–Wednesday 1200–1730. Charge. Telephone (01722) 335659. Also in Cathedral Close is the **Redcoats in the Wardrobe Military Museum**. Originally used as a storeroom by the Bishop, the building now contains a museum dedicated to the history of the Royal Gloucestershire, Berkshire and Wiltshire Regiment. Tearoom. Open April to October, daily 1000–1630; November, December, February and March, Tuesday–Sunday 1000–16030. Charge. Telephone (01722) 414536. The **Salisbury Museum** takes visitors on a journey through time, with displays that include artefacts from Stonehenge through to burial chambers and modern day Wedgwood pottery. Coffee shop. Open all year, Monday–Saturday 1000–1700; also Sunday in July and August. Charge. Telephone (01722) 332151. **Salisbury in Sound and Pictures**, located in a 13th-century medieval hall, is a 40 minute audio-visual presentation. Open April to September, daily 1100–1700. Charge. Telephone (01722) 412472.

Food and drink

Lots of places to chose from in Salisbury and Shaftesbury. There is a shop in Bower Chalke and two pubs in Bishopstone.

Coombe Nurseries Caravan Park
Ice creams and cold drinks for sale in the reception.

Roadside Lodge, Shaftesbury
Roadside café specializing in pizza. Open every day, early until late.

Fox and Goose, Coombe Bissett
Morning coffee and pub meals available. Outdoor seating.

Salisbury District Council's **Cycling & Walking Hotline** offers free information on cycling in the area (see page 8).

B Shaftesbury

Shaftesbury is an ancient Saxon hilltop town. **Shaftesbury Town Museum** is housed in a small cottage at the top of famous Gold Hill. Each room in the cottage contains many objects relating to the town's fascinating history and locality. The intriguing exhibits include a collection of Anglo-Saxon coins, a display of Dorset buttons and a wooden fire engine dating from 1744. Cottage garden alongside museum. Open Easter to end of September, daily 1100–1700. Charge. Telephone (01747) 852157. **Shaftesbury Abbey**, a Benedictine house for women, was founded circa 888 AD by King Alfred the great for his daughter Aethelgifu, the first abbess. The abbey acted as a catalyst for the prosperity of the town and surrounding area until the dissolution of the monasteries by Henry VIII in 1539. Many of the local houses are thought to be built partly of stone from the abbey ruins. The abbey remains have been excavated over the past 150 years. A **museum** contains a collection of carved stonework and medieval floor tiles. In the garden is a reconstructed Anglo Saxon herb bed. Open Easter to October, daily 1000–1700. Charge. Telephone (01747) 852910.

Route description

Start from Salisbury station, exit to mini roundabout and TR along Mill Road, no SP, passing Victoria Hotel on LHS. SO at next mini roundabout, SP Wiltshire Cycleway. SO at third mini roundabout and skirt public park to right. Enter centre of city. At traffic lights:

1   TR along High Street, no SP. Pass through large stone arch. TR at TJ in front of cathedral lawn, SP Military Museum/Medieval Hall/Salisbury Cathedral. Follow road as it bears left past cathedral on left and museums on right. TL at mini roundabout, through smaller stone arch, no SP.

2   TR at TJ, SP Avon Valley Path. Continue through traffic lights and over bridge to TR along Harnham Road, no SP.

3   TR at TJ, no SP. Pass telephone boxes on LHS, then TL along Old Blandford Road, no SP. Climb. At second entrance to Harnwood Road:

4   TR along Old Shaftesbury Drove Road, SP Byway. Continue on this rough grass track which gradually improves, passing racecourse. Continue SO when road comes in from left.

5   SO at XR (tarmac), SP Byway (8km/ 5 miles). Then LHF.

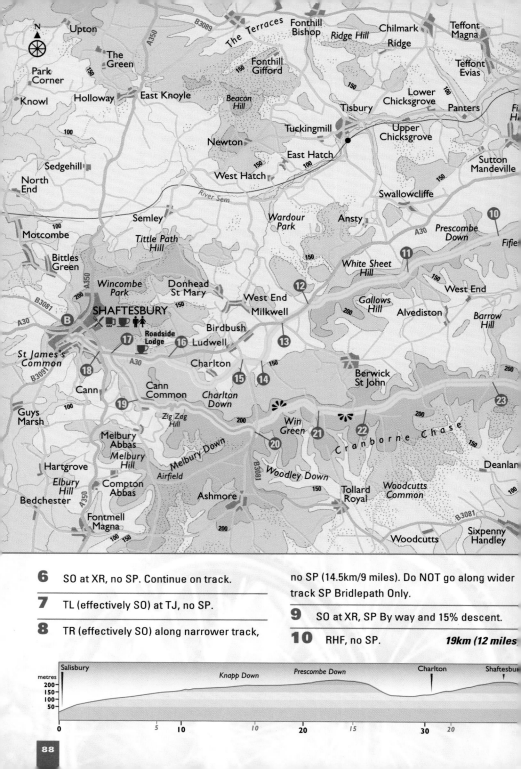

6 SO at XR, no SP. Continue on track.

7 TL (effectively SO) at TJ, no SP.

8 TR (effectively SO) along narrower track, no SP (14.5km/9 miles). Do NOT go along wider track SP Bridlepath Only.

9 SO at XR, SP By way and 15% descent.

10 RHF, no SP. **19km (12 miles**

Map labels (top to bottom, left to right):

Crouch's Down Baverstock · Barford Down · Grovely Hill · Chilhampton · Ford · Stratford sub Castle

River Avon · A345 · A36

Dinton · B3089 · Ditchampton · Fugglestone St Peter · A360 · A36

River Nadder · Barford St Martin · Ugford · A30 · WILTON · Burcombe · Bulbridge · Wilton Park · River Nadder · SALISBURY

Compton Wood · Compton Chamberlayne · Netherhampton · A3094 · **A** · **P** · **1**

Fovant · Compton Chamberlayne · Hoop Side · Harnham · **2** · **37**

8 · Knapp Down · **7** · Hydon Hill · Little Down · Netton Down · **6** · **5** · **4** · **36** · **3** · Britford

9 · Stoke Down · **29** The Pits · **30** · Stratford Tony · **31** · **35** · Odstock · Nunton

Broad Chalke · **25** · **26** Bishopstone · Coombe Nurseries Caravan Park · Fox and Goose · **34** · Odstock · A338

Knapp · Mount Sorrel · Stoke Farthing · **27** · Faulston Croucheston · **28** · Throope Hill · Coombe Bissett · **32** · **33** · Homington · Coombe Bissett Down · Odstock Down · Clearbury Down

Fifield Bavant · Knighton Hill · Stafford Tony Down · Hamington Down · Great Yews

Mead End · Bowerchalke · Woodminton · Misselfore · A354 · Little Toyd Down · Whitsbury Down · New Court Down

Vernditch Chase · Wick Down

24 · Martin Down · Rockbourne Down · Breamore Down · Breamore Wood

Woodyates · Martin · East Martin · Dunberry Hill · Whitsbury · North Street

A354 · Tidpit · Allen River · Rockbourne

Pentridge · Pentridge Hill · Crockerton Hill · Blackheath Down · North End · West Park · Scale — Mile / Km · A338

---

11 SO at XR, SP Byway. Steep descent to:

12 TL at XR (opposite Sands Lane), no SP (26.5km/16.5 miles). Enter Donhead St Andrew.

13 TL, SP (back to the way) Berwick St John/Alvediston. Immediately TR, no SP. Pass SP Except for Access.

14 TR at XR, SP Ludwell/Shaftesbury.

Elevation profile labels: Cranborne Chase · Woodminton · Bowerchalke · Mount Sorrel · Stoke Farthing · Croucheston · Bishopstone · Faulston · Stratford Tony · Coombe Bissett · Homington · Salisbury

feet — 655 — 490 — 330 — 165

kilometres — 25 · 30 · 50 · 35 · 60 · 40 · 70 · 45 · miles

15 SO at XR, SP Charlton.

16 TL at XR onto A30, no SP.

33km (20.5 miles)

17 If you wish to avoid Shaftesbury TL, SP Melbury Abbas and continue to direction 19, Otherwise, continue SO.

18 SO at roundabout, SP Town Centre. After visit, retrace to direction 17 where TR onto B3081, SP Melbury Abbas/Tollard Royal. Continue along this road to Cann Common.

19 TL, SP Tollard Royal/Sixpenny Handley (39.5km/24.5 miles). Continue through East Melbury and up Zig Zag Hill.

20 TL at XR, SP The Donheads. Then TR, SP Byway to Win Green. Continue along track to left of car park and skirt LHS of hill.

21 TL down short stretch of tarmac, by SP Byway to Tollard Royal. Immediately TR at TJ, SP Rushmore/Berwick St John. Follow SP Rushmore.

22 TL (effectively SO), SP Byway Ox Drove.

48km (30 miles)

23 SO at XR back onto tarmac, SP Handley.

24 TL at TJ, SP Bower Chalke/ Broadchalke/Salisbury, for quick descent – beware of right hand bend at the foot of hill. Enter Bowerchalke.

25 TR, SP Martin Blandford. Then TL at TJ, SP Salisbury, and TR along Knighton Road, SP Knighton/Stoke Farthing.

26 TR at TJ, SP Bishopstone.

27 TR along Flamstone Street, no SP.

28 TL at TJ along The Alley, no SP (64km/40 miles). Then TR along Netton Street, no SP. TR along Faulston, which turns into Mill Lane, no SP.

29 TR (effectively SO), SP Thorpe Manor Farm. Bear left passing staddlestones, ignoring bridleway on right. Arrive at circular tarmac road. TR at far corner, SP (in blue) Bridleway. Continue across grass to hedged track. Bear right at water to TL at TJ, no SP. Cross bridge to TR at TJ, no SP.

30 TR at XR, no SP (SP Racecourse opposite). Continue and enter Coombe Bissett.

31 TR at TJ, no SP. Pass Fox and Goose pub on LHS.

32 TL, SP Homington/Odstock. Continue into Homington.

33 TL, SP Village Only. Pass church on RHS.

34 TL (effectively SO) at TJ, no SP (71.5km/44.5 miles). Pass post box on LHS, bear left and climb.

35 TR at TJ, SP Salisbury. Then TL (next to Salisbury town SP). Climb.

36 TR at TJ, no SP. Then TL along Harnham Road Nos. 2–56, no SP. TL at TJ (traffic lights) along St Nicholas Road, no SP. Cross bridge. At large roundabout:

37 TL along Exeter Street, SP City Centre. When road splits take LHF. Pass High Street on LHS and return to the station and the end of the ride.

78km (48.5 miles)

Route information

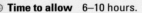 **Distance** 78.5km (49 miles)

Grade Moderate

Terrain Much of this ride is along the Inner Range Perimeter Path in the north of Salisbury Plain. The track is wide and well-surfaced, suitable for a mountain bike or strong touring bike.

Time to allow 6–10 hours.

Getting there by car Westbury is in west Wiltshire on the B3098, mid-way between Warminster and Trowbridge.

Getting there by train There is a railway station at Westbury. Telephone (0345) 484950 for travel information.

From Westbury the route heads east, climbing to Westbury White Horse and stunning views. The route then follows a wide and well-surfaced military road along the northern edge of Salisbury Plain for more extensive views before the route descends to the lanes around Woodborough. On past a second white horse at Alton Barnes as the route swings west towards the attractive town of Devizes and Caen Locks. Turning south, the route takes in Poulshot and Marston before heading back along the attractive B3098 to Westbury.

Places of interest along the route

A Westbury White Horse, Westbury
Remodelled on many occasions, the last in 1853, Westbury White Horse is 55m (180 feet) long and 33m (107 feet) high. The original horse was a likeness of Swallow, the horse that Alfred rode to victory against the Danes in 878. The likeness was lost in an enlargement in 1778. Free access at all reasonable times.

B Bratton Camp, Westbury Hill
A hillside fort defended by double banks and ditches, dating from the Iron Age. The barrow inside the camp is a burial mound of Neolithic age, dating from before 3000BC. English Heritage property. Free access at all reasonable times.

C Salisbury Plain
Covering an area of 32km (20 miles), Salisbury Plain is the largest chalk plateau in Britain. The plain was the home of the Great Bustard (a large bird now extinct) but today is mostly used by the armed forces. However, there are expansive views and a surprisingly large amount of wildlife.

D Alton Barnes White Horse, Alton Barnes
This white horse is 50m (165 feet) long and 55m (180 feet) high. A farmer commissioned the construction of the horse in 1812 but had to finish it himself when the designer disappeared with the 20 sovereign payment for the cutters.

E Devizes
Originally derived from the latin, *ad divisas*, meaning at the boundaries. Devizes is a pretty

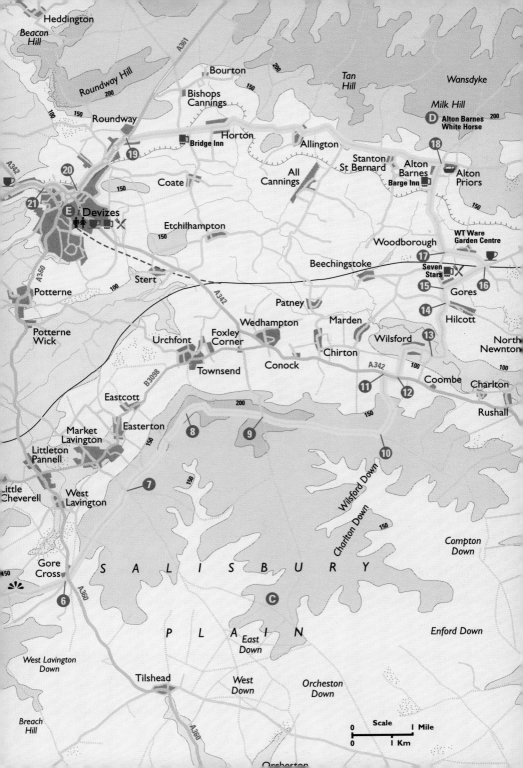

town full of Georgian architecture. The story of the town is depicted in the **Devizes Visitor Centre**. Here visitors are taken back to medieval times, when Devizes reputedly had the finest castle in Europe. Further exhibitions reveal the changes to the present day. Gift shop and Tourist Information Centre. Open summer, Monday–Saturday 0930–1700, Sunday 1030–1530; winter, Monday–Saturday 0930–1630. Admission free. Telephone (01380) 729408. The **Kennet and Avon Canal Museum** chronicles the history of the canal, from conception to building and ultimately restoration.Open all year, daily 1000–1700 (closes 1600 in winter). Charge. Telephone (01380) 721279. One of the greatest engineering feats on the canal are the **Caen Hill Locks** (on the west side of Devizes) – a flight of 29 locks rising 72m (236 feet). The locks were re-opened in 1990 following extensive restoration.

Route description

Leave Westbury station to TR (effectively SO) at TJ opposite Railway Inn. Pass under railway and SO at roundabout, SP Warminster/Frome/Town Centre. SO at next roundabout along Hayes Road for 400m, SP Poole/Warminster. TL at TJ along Warminster Road, SP Bratton.

1 TR at XR along Newton, SP White Horse. Pass chapel/pottery on LHS and climb through residential area. Leave Westbury, take LHF after stables and keep climbing. LHF at top of hill keeping to tarmac, SP Byway. Pass entrance to Westbury White Horse and Bratton Camp on LHS.

2 TR at TJ onto well-graded track, no SP (4.5km/3 miles). After 400m arrive farm buildings on LHS – bear left around these and continue with Salisbury Plain on RHS (with frequent no access SP).

3 TR at TJ, no SP, but SP No Vehicles over 4 Ton on LHS (8km/5 miles). Follow track for short distance to LHF in front of army range building (SP on building VP6 Bratton, GR929508). Continue for climb. RHF, SP Byway. Pass trig point on RHS.

4 TL (effectively SO) at TJ, no SP. Leave tarmac.

5 TL at XR, no SP (enter military compound if TR), back onto tarmac.

6 TL at TJ for 100m, no SP (18.5km/11.5 miles). SO at XR, SP C.O.T.E.C. Lavington.

7 SO at XR off-road, no SP (army building to right of junction – VP11 Lavington GR024534).

8 RHF in front of large copse, no SP (24km/15 miles). Pass flagpole and oil tank on RHS.

9 SO at XR, no SP. Pass army building (VP12 Redhorn GR060554) on RHS. Note: the next junction is the trickiest of the route – pass a large orange cone on RHS, then pass between small copse on LHS and larger one on RHS. After 500m pass another copse on LHS, SP Private/Keep Out. After further 300m:

10 TL, no SP (29.5km/18.5 miles). Follow grassy track for 200m as it passes through fence via two metal gates (SP landrover and tank at gates). Continue for 200m to pass to right of large green corrugated barn and descend, bearing left to pass another barn on RHS before further descent.

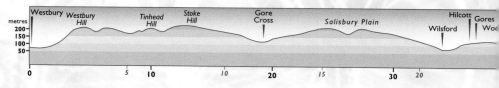

11 TR at TJ, no SP. **32km (20 miles)**

12 TL, SP Wilsford. Continue through Wilsford.

13 TL at TJ, no SP. Pass Cuttenham Farm on LHS and enter Hilcott.

14 TL at TJ, SP Woodborough.

15 TR, SP Bottlesford/Pewsey. Pass Seven Stars pub on LHS.

16 To visit WT Ware Garden Centre TR for 200m. Otherwise, TL at TJ, SP Woodborough/Alton and enter Woodborough.

17 TR at XR along Honey Street, SP Alton/Honey Street (39.5km/24.5 miles). Cross canal and continue into Alton Barnes.

18 TL, SP Stanton St Bernard/Devizes. Continue to pass Alton Barnes White Horse on RHS and cross canal twice more.

19 SO at large roundabout, SP Devizes (51.5km/32 miles). SO at next two roundabouts. Cross canal.

20 TR at roundabout opposite church. TR at next roundabout. Cross pedestrian crossing and bear left to SO at mini roundabout, SP Through Traffic. At next roundabout bear right along New Park Street.

21 TR at mini roundabout, SP Trowbridge/Chippenham/Bath (54.5km/34 miles). To avoid towpath, SO at next mini roundabout, cross canal and continue on this road (becomes dual carriageway). Otherwise, road crosses top of Caen Hill Locks – take towpath on LHS and follow to foot of locks, passing Lock Cottage Tearooms on RHS on the way down. Pass under small bridge and follow short path back to road. TR at TJ opposite Foxhangers House,

no SP. Arrive dual carriageway and TR at TJ, SP Trowbridge.

22 TL, SP Poulshot/Worton/Bulkington. Continue through Poulshot.

23 TL at TJ, SP Worton.

24 TR, SP Marston (63.5km/39.5 miles). Continue through Marston and Coulston.

25 TR at TJ, no SP. Pass Baynton Farm on RHS. Continue through Edington and Bratton into Westbury.

26 TR, SP station and return to station and end of route. **78.5km (49 miles)**

Food and drink

Plenty of choice in Westbury and Devizes, and convenience stores, pubs and a tearoom in Bratton. Refreshments are also available at Caen Hill Lock (tearoom half-way down the flight).

Seven Stars, Gores
Pub and Egon Ronay-rated restaurant.

WT Ware Garden Centre Coffee Shop, Woodborough
A CTC-listed coffee shop.

Barge Inn, Alton Barnes
On the Kennet and Avon Canal. Open all day. Garden.

Bridge Inn, Horton
Lunchtime and evening meals available.

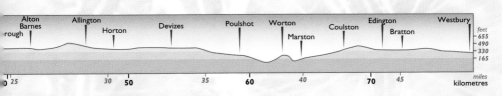

Route information

Distance 82km (51 miles)

Grade Moderate

Terrain Quiet lanes and country roads with a number of climbs, although nothing severe.

Time to allow 5–8 hours.

Getting there by car Frome is south of Bath on the A362. There is long-term parking (pay and display) in the centre of town – follow SP Tourist Information.

Getting there by train There is a railway station at Frome. Telephone (0345) 484950 for travel information.

The attractive town of Frome provides the start point, from where the route meanders south past the unusual castle at Nunney to Trudoxhil. A climb takes you on to the isolated settlement of Gare Hill. On through Stourhead, Zeals and Bourton to the southerly point of the ride at Wincanton. Turning north, the route takes you through a series of delightful villages to Cranmore, home to the East Somerset railway. The tearoom here will set you up nicely for the return to Frome.

Places of interest along the route

A Frome

Frome's origins lie, as with most Somerset towns, in the cloth industry. Today it is the fourth largest town in Somerset and contains the largest number of listed buildings of a town in Somerset. **Frome Museum,** close to the Tourist Information Centre, contains many exhibits on local history, including collections of photographs, a 17th-century fire engine and a reconstructed chemist shop. Open all year, Wednesday–Saturday 1000–1600. Nominal charge. Telephone (01373) 467271.

B Nunney Castle

Built in 1373 by Sir John de la Mere, Nunney Castle is based on the castles Sir John saw whilst fighting alongside the Black Prince in south west France. The castle was damaged and abandoned after a short siege during the Civil War. Parliament then decreed that its roof and internal structures be removed. Today, the castle is a reasonably well-preserved ruin surrounded by a moat. English Heritage property. Free access at all reasonable times.

C Stourhead House and Gardens

The fine Palladian house was designed in 1721 for Henry Hoare. Laid out between 1741 and 1780, the gardens provide an ever changing series of vistas across a central lake. Mock temples and follies adorn the shore as well-

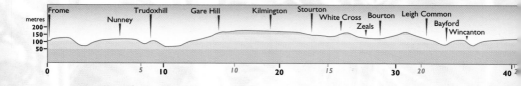

	Frome		Trudoxhill	Gare Hill		Kilmington	Stourton		Bourton	Leigh Common	
metres		Nunney						White Cross	Zeals		Bayford
200											Wincanton
150											
100											
50											

| 0 | 5 | 10 | 10 | 20 | 15 | 30 | 20 | 40 |

maintained paths guide visitors around the grounds. Excellent tearoom. National Trust property. House open April to October, Tuesday–Friday 1400–1730, weekends 1130–1730. Garden open all year, daily 0900–1900 (or dusk if earlier). Charge. Telephone (01747) 841152.

D East Somerset Railway

Founded in 1974 by the wildlife artist David Shepherd, the East Somerset Railway is on the site of a railway, opened in 1858, which ran between Wells and Witham Junction. Visitors can see the preserved station, take a ride on a steam train and see an exhibition of David Shepherd's work. Another excellent tearoom (admission free). Open all year, daily from 1030; closing times vary. Charge. Telephone (01749) 880417.

Food and drink

Lots of choice in Frome and Wincanton. There is a pub at Stourhead and convenience stores in Zeals and Bayford.

White Hart Inn, Trudoxhill
Pub offering home-cooked food.

Bell and Groom, Zeals
Pub offering morning coffee and meals.

Lamb Inn, Upton Noble
Food served 1200–1400.

Three Horseshoes, Batcombe
Pub meals available.

Route description

Start from Frome railway station. Exit to TL at TJ opposite Wallbridge, no SP. RHF at traffic lights, SP Radstock/Town Centre. Gently climb to TR at TJ opposite Wesley Methodist Church, SP Radstock. TL at mini roundabout, SP Radstock.

1 TL along Nunney Road, SP Nunney/Shepton Mallet. Enter Nunney. To visit Nunney Castle pass Praters (house name) on RHS and TR, cross stream and continue SO to entrance. Otherwise, continue SO through Nunney.

2 TL (effectively SO), SP Subway. Pass to left of Theobald Arms, to go under A361.

3 TL at TJ, no SP (8km/5 miles). Continue through Trudoxhill, following SP Gare Hill as road climbs, passing church on LHS. Road flattens out in woodland.

4 TR (effectively SO) at TJ, SP Bruton.
16km (10 miles)

5 TL (effectively SO) at XR, SP Kilmington/Stourhead.

6 TR at TJ, SP Stourhead/Mere.

7 TR, SP Stourhead/Stourton. Continue through Stourton and Stourhead into Zeals, passing Stourhead House and Gardens.

8 TL at TJ for 50m, SP Bourton (26.5km/16.5 miles). TR, SP Penselwood. Then immediately TL along Tulse Hill, SP Penselwood. Leave Zeals and:

9 TL for 50m, SP Bourton. TR, no SP. Pass King's Green on LHS.

10 TR at TJ, no SP. Pass Stobrick Cottage on RHS. Continue through Bayford and into Wincanton. Pass Tourist Information Centre/Toilets on RHS. As road goes left to enter one way system, dismount and walk SO for 50m (avoiding long circuit of town). Then:

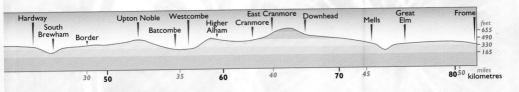

11 TR along North Street, SP Race Course (35.5km/22 miles). Pass racecourse on LHS.

12 TR, SP Charlton Musgrove/Gillingham/Mere. Then immediately TR at TJ, no SP.

13 TL, no SP (39.5km/24.5 miles). Pass Stoke Farm on LHS.

14 TL, SP South Brewham/North Brewham.

15 TR at TJ opposite post box, no SP. Enter South Brewham and climb out of village.

16 TR at TJ, SP Kilmington/Warminster.

17 TL, SP Upton Noble/Witham Friary (48km/30 miles). Enter Upton Noble.

18 TR at XR, SP Wanstrow/Frome.

19 SO at XR, SP Eastcombe. Descend through woods.

20 TR at TJ, no SP (54.5km/34 miles). Enter Batcombe (no SP) and continue through village to bear right. Road is flat then climbs and descends past Alham Farm and East Somerset Railway on LHS.

21 TR, no SP (62km/38.5 miles). Pass Strode Arms on LHS.

22 SO at XR across A361, SP Downhead. Climb and enter Downhead.

23 SO at XR, SP Leigh Upon Mendip/Coleford.

24 TR, SP Mells/Frome.

25 TL at XR, SP Chantry/Frome/Mells. Enter Mells.

26 TL, SP Vobster/Radstock. Almost immediately TL at TJ, no SP, and descend.

27 TR at TJ, no SP (small river on LHS).

28 TL, no SP (72.5km/45 miles). Pass SP Except for Access.

29 TR at TJ opposite stone bus shelter, no SP. Pass Talbot Inn on LHS.

30 Arrive five-way XR and take second TL, SP Great Elm/Frome.

31 TR at TJ, no SP. Then TL, SP Warminster/Shepton Mallet.

32 TR, no SP. Pass Farmers Arms pub on LHS. Enter Frome (no SP).

33 TR at TJ, no SP (next to SP Welshmill Road). Descend into centre of town. To complete the route at the Tourist Information Centre/car park, TR along Bridge Street. Otherwise, continue SO.

34 TL at TJ for 10m, SP Warminster. Then TL, SP station. Descend to TL at TJ, SP Warminster and TR into the station to complete the ride. ***82km (51 miles)***

Nunney Castle

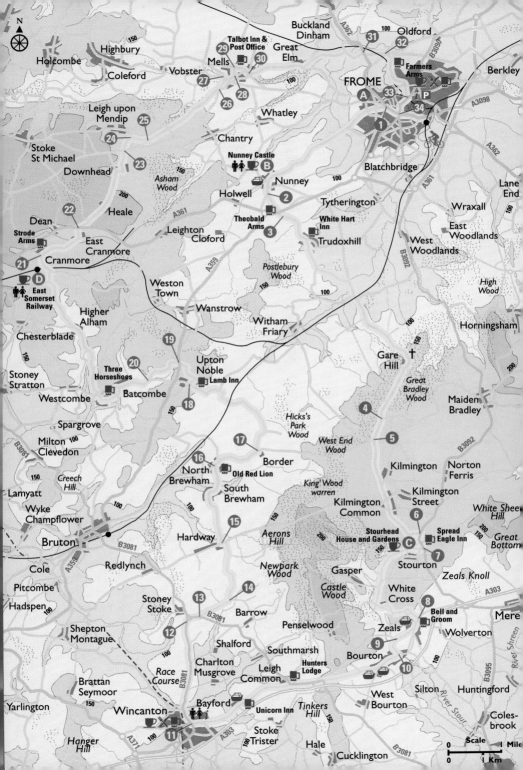

SALISBURY PLAIN AND THE WYLYE VALLEY

Route information

Distance   87km (54 miles)

Grade   Moderate

Terrain   Tarmac roads throughout. The first part of the route involves gentle climbing across Salisbury Plain and there is one short climb later in the route.

Time to allow   5–9 hours.

Getting there by car   Warminster is on the A36. There is free long-term car parking next to the Tourist Information Centre.

Getting there by train   There is a railway station at Warminster. Telephone (0345) 484950 for travel information.

From Warminster, the route follows the line of the railway to Heytesbury, from where it turns north east to cross Salisbury Plain for extensive views and evidence of army activity. On through the army town of Larkhill before heading south through the pretty town of Amesbury. The route follows the River Avon along a delightful valley for a short sharp climb and descent into Wilton. The last section of the route takes you back to Warminster through the Wylye Valley, popular with cyclists.

Route description

Start from Warminster railway station and cycle towards town along The Avenue, which changes to Station Road. TL at roundabout (opposite National Westminster Bank), SP Salisbury (A36).

1   SO at roundabout, SP Heytesbury/Norton Bavant. Leave Warminster with railway on LHS.

2   SO at roundabout, SP Heytesbury. Enter Heytesbury, pass Angel Inn and follow road left, SP Main Road.

3   TR along Park Street, no SP. Pass football club on LHS and TL (effectively SO) along Park Lane. At end pass through bollards (next to mile post) to cycle along narrow path to rejoin A36.

4   TL, SP Chitterne (8km/5 miles). Climb for extensive views across Salisbury Plain. Enter Chitterne.

5   TL, SP Tilshead. Pass attractive church on RHS. Continue into Tilshead.

6   TR at TJ, SP Salisbury/Shrewton (20km/12.5 miles). Just before post office:

7   TL along Candown Road, no SP. Follow this road as it bears right, passing Easthill Cottage on RHS. Continue climbing as road swings around army camp. Pass several tank crossings.

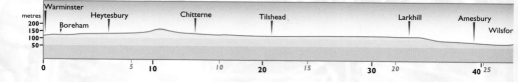

Heale House

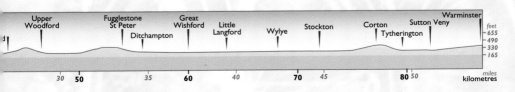

Old Dilton

Upton Scudamore

Warminster Down

Summer Down

West Lavington Down

Boreham Down

S a l i s b u r y

Breach Hill

P l a i n

Battlesbury Hill

WARMINSTER

Boreham

Scratchbury Hill

Catley Hill

Knook Down

Kings Head

Chitterne

Bishopstrow

Norton Bavant

Anstey Hill

Codford Down

Crockerton

Heytesbury

Red Lion/ Angel Inn

Shear Cross

Sutton Veny

Woolpack

Knook

Tytherington

Upton Lovell

Corton

Longbridge Deverill

Codford St. Peter

Codford St. Mary

Brixton Deverill

Tytherington Hill

Corton Hill

Boyton

Sherrington

Fisherton de la Mere

Stockton

River Wylye

Bell

Monkton Deverill

Corton Down

W y l y e

Bapton

G r e a t   R i d g e

Stony Hill

Pen Hill

Pertwood

Stockton Wood

Keysley Down

Bockerly Hill

Chicklade

Chilmark Down

Teffont Down

Middle

Berwick St Leonard

Fonthill Bishop

West Knoyle

Hindon

The Terraces

Ridge Hill

Chilmark

Teffont Magna

Upton

The Green

Scale

Fonthill Gifford

Ridge

Teffont Evias

Holloway

Beacon Hill

Lower Chicksgrove

River Nadder

East Knoyle

Tisbury

0   1 Mile

0   1 Km

Rose and Crown **7**

Tilshead

6

Tilshead Camp

West Down

Orcheston Down

Netheravon

N

Figheldean

Ablington

A345

100

Milston

B3085

Durrington

Orcheston

8

Bustard Inn

Knighton Down

10

Stonehenge Inn

B3086

Maddington

Shrewton

9

Larkhill

11

A3028

Bulford

Rollestone

100

Woodhenge **B**

12

B3083

Countess

A344

14

Amesbury

West Amesbury

15

13

Winterbourne Stoke

A303

B3083

100

A360

Normanton

Wilsford

River Avon

Berwick St James

Lake

Great Durnford

100

Uppington

Bridge at Woodford

Upper Woodford

100

Wylye

V

100

Steeple Langford

A36

Stapleford

Middle Woodford

Netton

Heale House & Gardens **C**

Hanging Langford

Little Langford

150

Salterton

A345

Winterbourne Dauntsey

Gravel Wood

Royal Oak

21

Stoford

Wheatsheaf Inn

Lower Woodford

Winterbourne Earls

Hills

Great Wishford

South Newton

Little Durnford

Hurdcott

Ford

River Bourne

A338

Crouch's Down

100

Baverstock

150

Heath Wood

Grovely Hill

River Wylye

A36

Chilhampton

17

16

100

A360

River Avon

Stratford sub Castle

100

Dinton

B3089

Barford Down

Ditchampton

100

18

Fugglestone St Peter

Laverstock

Barford St Martin

Ugford

20

D

SALISBURY

A30

Wilton

19

Wilton House

A36

Burcombe

Bulbridge

103

8 TR at roundabout, no SP (28km/17.5 miles). Immediately pass Bustard Inn on RHS.

9 TL at XR, SP Larkhill Garrison.

10 TR at roundabout for 200m, SP Salisbury/Amesbury (35.5km/22 miles). TR, SP Public Footpath, and walk short distance until footpath becomes road. Follow road and TL (effectively SO) at TJ (Woodhenge on RHS).

11 TR at TJ along Countess Road, no SP. Enter Amesbury.

12 SO at roundabout, SP Town Centre/Boscombe Down/Salisbury. Continue SO through traffic lights.

13 TR at roundabout, SP Town centre. Pass shops on either side.

14 TL at TJ along Church Street, SP West Amesbury the Woodfords. Pass church on RHS. Pass picnic site (bench) on LHS.

15 TL, SP Woodford/Salisbury/Heale Gardens (40km/25 miles). Continue along this beautiful valley road, through Upper, Middle and Lower Woodford. Pass Heale Gardens on LHS.

16 TR, SP Wilton (50.5km/31.5 miles). Climb steeply out of valley.

17 SO at XR, SP Wilton.

18 To visit Wilton House, TL at large roundabout. Otherwise, SO, SP Shaftesbury/Wilton House.

19 SO at XR (traffic lights) along West Street, no SP.

20 TR, SP Great Wishford (55.5km/34.5 miles). This is the start of Wylye Valley. Continue into Great Wishford.

21 SO at XR, SP Little Langford/Hanging Langford/Wylye. Continue through Hanging Langford into Wylye.

22 TR at XR along Sheepwash Lane, no SP but opposite turn for Dinton (68.5km/42.5 miles). Continue on this narrow path that quickly swings left. Pass church on RHS.

23 TL at TJ, no SP. Pass shop on LHS. Continue through Boyton and Sutton Veny.

24 TL at large roundabout, SP Warminster (84.5km/52.5 miles). Continue into town centre and TR to station and the end of the ride.

87km (54 miles)

Places of interest along the route

A Warminster

Dating from Saxon times, Warminster later became an important centre for trading in cloth, wool and corn. There are many old buildings of local stone including three inns whose upper stories are supported across the pavement by pillars. Some of Warminster's textile history is illustrated in **Dents Glove Museum** whose collection dates back to the 16th century. Open by appointment only. Telephone (01985) 212291. Situated within Warminster Library, the **Dewey Museum** is the personal archive of H.N. Dewey. Monthly displays show off the collection of local and natural history and geology. Open all year, daily. Telephone (01985) 215640. Warminster's military connections are reflected in the **Infantry and Small Arms School Corps Weapons Museum** which is located on MOD property. An appointment is necessary to view this comprehensive collection of military firearms. Telephone (01985) 842487.

B Woodhenge, near Amesbury

Discovered in 1926 through aerial photographs, Woodhenge was a Bronze Age wooden structure comprising of six concentric, oval rings, within a bank and outer ditch. The long axis of the rings point to the rising sun on Midsummer Day. In the centre is the grave of a child. Today the structure has long gone but the site of the timber uprights are marked by concrete posts. Free access at all reasonable times.

C Heale House and Gardens, Netton

Sitting beside the River Avon, much of the house is unchanged since King Charles II hid here for five days in 1651, following the battle of Worcester. The surrounding 3ha (8 acres) of gardens are centred around an authentic Japanese teahouse and nikko bridge. Also plant centre and shop (admission free) selling unusual plants and shrubs. Light refreshments are available on a DIY basis in the plant centre. Open all year, daily 1000–1700. Charge. Telephone (01722) 782504.

D Wilton

Once the county town of Wiltshire, Wilton is now more famous for its carpets. This heritage is depicted in the **Wilton Carpet Factory**, where visitors can see both Axminster and Wilton carpets being produced on looms. Open all year, Monday–Saturday 1015–1545, Sunday 1115–1545. Charge. Telephone (01722) 744919. Next door is Wilton Shopping Village, incorporating the **Town Museum**. Admission free. and a café. Wilton House is situated in 8.5ha (21 acres) of grounds, **Wilton House** was given to William Herbert by Henry V111 in 1541. Almost destroyed by fire in 1647, the present house was rebuilt by Inigo Jones. Inside visitors can see a substantial art collection, including works by Rubens and Van Dyke. Also Tudor kitchen, the magnificent cube room, 19th-century model

soldiers, a massive adventure playground and a film theatre. Special events held during summer. Café. Open Easter to October, daily 1100–1800 (last admission 1700). Charge. Telephone (01722) 743115.

Food and drink

Plenty of choice in Warminster and Amesbury. Refreshments are also available at Heale House and Gardens, Wilton Shopping Village and Wilton House. Pubs and convenience stores are passed throughout the route.

Red Lion, Heytesbury
Pub with pleasant riverside garden.

Kings Head, Chitterne
An attractive pub noted for the decorative wheel and hanging baskets. Morning coffee, bar meals and garden.

Rose and Crown, Tilshead
Thatched pub with interior exposed wooden beams. Pub meals available.

Bustard Inn, near Tilshead
Good food and pleasant garden seating.

The Bridge at Woodford, Upper Woodford
Pub featuring a delightful riverside seating area.

THE GRANDE RANDONNÉE

Route information

Distance   141km (88 miles)

Grade   Moderate

Terrain   Tarmac roads throughout and several long hills, notably Cheddar Gorge, but nothing too severe.

Time to allow   1–2 days.

Getting there by car   Bath can be reached from the A4, A46 and A36. There are several pay and display car parks in the city. For free long-term parking use the western end of Victoria Park.

Getting there by train   Bath Spa is the nearest railway station. Telephone (0345) 484950 for travel information.

From Bath the route heads north west to Saltford. On west through small villages to the Chew Valley and the delightful Chew Lake. Climbing to the Northern Mendips, the route traverses the hillside offering glimpses of Blagdon Lake before arriving at Churchill. On through Winscombe and Bleadon to the seaside resort of Brean (a good place to stay overnight if tackling this route over two days). The route back to Bath takes in the two very different sides of Somerset's geography, first over the Somerset Levels through Mark and Blackford, before climbing through Cheddar

Gorge into the Mendip Hills. The final section into Bath follows quiet lanes through attractive villages.

Route description

Starting at Bath Spa station, head past the Royal Hotel RHS, and the bus station LHS, initially walking the first 20m. SO at traffic lights to bear left, passing Bath Abbey LHS. Immediately bear left in front of church to pass Guildhall RHS. Climb passing Postal Museum LHS. At traffic lights, TL at XR, SP Bristol/Hospital. After 400m the road bears left, 20m after this TR along Queen's Parade Place to enter Royal Victoria Park between two pillars. Cycle through park admiring Royal Crescent RHS.

1   TL at XR opposite Obelisk, no SP. Descend and TR at TJ (opposite Albion Place), no SP. Pass large playground on RHS. SO at traffic lights, SP Bath Spa University College. Shortly:

2   TL along Locksbrook Road, SP Locksbrook. SO at mini roundabout, no SP. Pass Bike Shop LHS.

3   TL onto Bristol & Bath Railway Path (4km/2.5 miles), SP Bristol, and continue. Arrive at sculpture (signed Saltford) on bridge:

4   TR, no SP, and descend narrow track. TL at TJ, no SP, and pass under railway path. Pass Bird in Hand pub on LHS. TL along Beech Road, no SP but opposite Stone Cross.

5   SO at XR along Manor Road. Follow road as it bears right then bears right again. TL along narrow lane (effectively SO), SP National Cycleway 3.

6 TL at TJ along Montague Road, no SP (10.5km/6.5 miles). Then TL (effectively SO) and pass Little Orchard on RHS. Pass Manor Barn and TR at TJ, no SP. Continue along this narrow, windy road, into residential area.

7 TL at TJ, no SP. Then TR, SP Chewton/Compton Dando. Descend.

8 TR, SP Queen Charlton. Climb steeply.

9 TL at XR, SP Whitchurch.

14.5km (9 miles)

10 TR at TJ, SP Whitchurch/Pensford. TL along Hursley Lane, no SP. Pass SP Unsuitable for Wide Vehicles.

11 TR at TJ onto A37, no SP, then TL along Gibbet Lane, no SP.

12 TL at TJ, no SP. *18.5km (11.5 miles)*

13 TL, SP public telephone. Continue through Norton Malreward and descend.

14 TR at TJ, no SP. Continue past TL for Stanton Drew into Chew Magna.

15 TL into Tunbridge Road, SP Bishop Sutton/Bath. Pass fire station on RHS.

16 TR along Denny Lane, SP Avon Cycleway. *25km (15.5 miles)*

17 To visit Chew Valley Lake TL at TJ for 100m, then TR (25.5km/16 miles). Otherwise, TR at TJ, no SP. Pass reservoir towers on LHS.

18 TL at TJ, SP Cheddar. TR along Breach Hill Lane, SP Breach Hill/Nempnett. Climb to pass obelisk on RHS. Continue, following SP Nempnett. Just after telephone on RHS:

19 TL, no SP. SO at XR, SP Butcombe/Blagdon. *32km (20 miles)*

20 TL, no SP. Descend passing high voltage electric cables. Take LHF, no SP (opposite wall). Then TL at TJ, SP Blagdon.

35km (21.5 miles)

21 TR, SP Aldwick.

22 TL (effectively SO) at TJ, no SP. Pass Bourne Lane on LHS. TR at TJ onto A30, SP Weston-Super-Mare/Bristol. Then TR along narrow, high-hedged lane. Pass SP Except for Access.

23 SO at XR across A38, no SP (Langford Place on RHS). *41km (25.5 miles)*

24 TL at mini roundabout, SP Churchill/Cheddar. Then TR at TJ onto A38, SP Taunton/Exeter. Continue into Churchill.

25 TR at traffic lights onto A368, SP Weston-Super-Mare/Churchill Sports Centre/ Banwell. Pass Nelson Arms pub on LHS and TR, no SP (in front of clock tower). Pass between SP Except for Access. Pass methodist church on RHS.

26 TL at TJ, no SP (46.5km/29 miles). SO at XR into Hill Road, no SP. Climb.

27 TL (effectively SO) at TJ. Cross pedestrian crossing and TR along The Lynch, no SP. Pass Oldfield on LHS, and follow road as it bears right and crosses bridge.

28 TL at TJ, no SP (50km/31 miles). Pass Oakland RHS and shortly afterwards TR into Barton Road, SP Barton/Loxton.

29 TR at XR, SP Loxton/Weston-Super-Mare. Pass Forgotton World on RHS. Cross M5 and enter Loxton.

30 TL, SP Bleadon/Weston-Super-Mare (55km/34 miles). Enter Bleadon (no SP) and bear left in village.

31 SO at XR, SP Model Motor Racing Circuit/Animal Farm Country Park (60km/37.5 miles). Cross A370. Pass Anchor Inn on LHS. Continue along Accommodation Road. Cross railway and continue with railway on LHS.

32 TR, SP Brean/Berrow (63.5km/39.5 miles). Recross railway. Continue, passing Animal Farm Country Park on LHS.

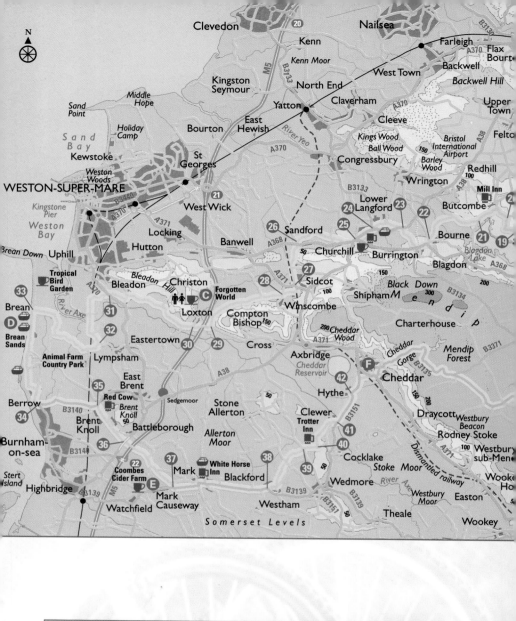

N

WESTON-SUPER-MARE

Clevedon
Nailsea
Kenn
Kenn Moor
Farleigh
Flax
Bourt
Backwell
West Town
Backwell Hill
Kingston
Seymour
North End
Claverham
Upper
Town
Yatton
Cleeve
Felto
East
Hewish
Bourton
Kings Wood
Ball Wood
Bristol
International
Airport
Barley
Wood
Redhill
Sand
Point
Holiday
Camp
Middle
Hope
Sand
Bay
Kewstoke
St
Georges
Congresbury
Wrington
Mill Inn
Weston
Woods
West Wick
Lower
Langford
Butcombe
Kingstone
Pier
Bourne
Weston
Bay
Locking
Sandford
Churchill
Burrington
Blagdon
Brean Down
Uphill
Hutton
Banwell
Sidcot
Blagdon
Lake
Tropical
Bird
Garden
Bleadon
Hill
Christon
Forgotten
World
Winscombe
Shipham
Black Down
Mendip
Brean
Bleadon
Loxton
Compton
Bishop
Charterhouse
Brean
Sands
Eastertown
Cross
Cheddar
Wood
Mendip
Forest
Animal Farm
Country Park
Lympsham
Axbridge
Cheddar
Gorge
Cheddar
East
Brent
Cheddar
Reservoir
Hythe
Draycott
Westbury
Beacon
Rodney Stoke
Berrow
Red Cow
Brent
Knoll
Sedgemoor
Stone
Allerton
Clewer
Trotter
Inn
Cocklake
Westbury
sub-Men
Burnham-
on-sea
Brent
Knoll
Battleborough
Allerton
Moor
Stoke Moor
Wedmore
Wook
Ho
Stert
Island
Highbridge
Coombes
Cider Farm
Mark
White Horse
Inn
Blackford
Westbury
Moor
Easton
Wook
Ho
Watchfield
Mark
Causeway
Westham
Theale
Wookey
Somerset Levels

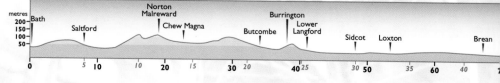

metres
200
150
100
50

Bath
Saltford
Norton
Malreward
Chew Magna
Butcombe
Burrington
Lower
Langford
Sidcot
Loxton
Brean

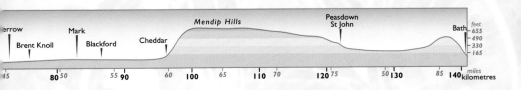

33 TL at TJ, SP Leisure Centre/Berrow/Burnham. Continue and SO at roundabout, no SP. *70km (43.5 miles)*

34 TL along Brent Road, SP B3140/Bristol (74km/46 miles). Enter Brent Knoll.

35 TR along Brent Street, SP Brent Knoll/Mark/Highbridge.

36 SO at XR, SP Mark (79km/49 miles) – cross dual carriageway with care using central reservation. Pass Coombes Cider Farm.

37 TL at XR onto BB3139, SP Wells/Mark/Wedmore. Continue through Mark into Blackford.

38 TL (effectively SO), SP Stoughton/Allerton (87km/54 miles). Enter Stoughton.

39 TL at TJ, SP Chapel Allerton/Weare (90km/56 miles). Then TR, no SP (opposite post box). Pass Pear Tree Farm on LHS. Enter Crickham. TL (effectively SO), no SP. Pass Crickham Baptist Church on RHS. Good view SO.

40 TL at TJ, no SP, for steep descent.

41 TL at TJ along centrally-lined road, no SP. Cross bridge with metal railings and continue SO towards Cheddar Gorge.

42 TR, SP Cheddar/Wells/Leisure Centre/Business Park/Recycling Centre. TR at TJ (next to war memorial), SP Wells/Cheddar Gorge. TL, SP Cheddar Gorge. Pass to left of stone market cross. Then SO at roundabout, SP Cheddar Cheese Co/Cheddar Gorge and Caves/Tourist Information (96.5km/60 miles). Continue on this road (B3135) through Cheddar Gorge and over the Mendips.

43 TL (effectively SO), no SP but pass between SP Right Hand Bend (109.5km/68 miles). Continue along this wooded road. Pass Chetwon Cheese Dairy on LHS.

44 SO at XR along Chapel Hill, SP Emborough.

45 TL at TJ onto B3139, SP Chilcompton/Bath. *115.5km (72 miles)*

46 TR at TJ SP Yeovil/South Mallet. Then TL, SP Radstock/Bath/Trowbridge/Old Down Chilcompton. Enter Chilcompton. TL, SP Clapton. Continue on this road towards Midsomer Norton.

47 TR at TJ, no SP (large mining slag heap on LHS). TL at XR, no SP (122km/76 miles), and climb lane.

48 SO at XR along Monger Lane, no SP. Then TL (effectively SO), no SP. Climb gently, passing under high voltage cables.

49 TR at TJ, no SP (124km/77 miles). Pass under high voltage cables and continue along lane for steep climb.

50 SO at XR, no SP. TL at XR, no SP. Enter Peasedown St John.

51 TL, SP Peasedown St John. Pass school and shops on RHS. Just before telephone box on LHS, TL and descend Keels Hill, no SP.

52 TR at TJ, no SP (opposite Chapel View), for descent (130km/81 miles). TR, no SP (just before road rises). Pass fenced in trees on RHS.

53 TR at TJ, no SP. Then TL, SP Combe Hay.

54 TR at TJ, no SP (opposite bollards). Then TL at XR, SP Bath, for gradual climb.

55 TL at TJ, SP Radstock/City Centre (136km/85 miles). Then TR at large roundabout, SP Bath/City Centre. Enter Bath. SO at large roundabout, SP City Centre. Descend.

56 SO at large roundabout, SP City Centre. Cross river and immediately TR, SP City Centre. Pass car park on LHS. Bear left at traffic lights, pass bus station on RHS and TR at TJ, no SP, to finish the ride at the station. *141km (88 miles)*

Places of interest along the route

Ⓐ Bath
Renowned as a World Heritage City. See route 11 for details.

Ⓑ Chew Valley Lake
The lake at Chew Valley was created as a reservoir in the 1950s and adds much to the beauty of the area. It is popular with fishermen and sailors. Shoreside walks. Visitor Centre and tearoom with great views of the lake. Free access to lake at all reasonable times. Tearoom open daily 1030–1730. Telephone (01275) 332339.

Ⓒ Forgotton World, Loxton
A living museum. Visitors can learn about the skill of the wheelwright and discover the life of a Romany. Also Old Tyme Victorian Fair. Tearoom. Open 1000–1800: Easter to October, Wednesday–Sunday; July, August and Bank Holidays, daily. Charge. Telephone (01934) 750841.

Ⓓ Brean
On the Bristol Channel, Brean is a popular holiday centre. There are fairground attractions, golf and a leisure centre with a swimming pool. The **Tropical Bird Garden**, at the northern end of Brean, was established in 1972 and contains over 30 species of birds from all over the world. Licenced café. Shop. Open April to October, daily 0900–dusk. Charge. Telephone (01278) 751209. **Animal Farm Country Park** offers plenty of opportunities to see and touch a variety of animals. Telephone (01278) 751628.

Ⓔ Coombes Cider Farm, near Mark
An opportunity to sample the local speciality. See route 20 for further details.

Food and drink

Plenty of choice in Bath and Churchill. There are numerous tearooms and pubs passed en route and refreshments are also available at the places of interest.

🍴 Bird in Hand, Saltford
Good pub meals served. Garden.

🍴 Red Cow, Brent Knoll
Pub meals available.

Ⓕ Cheddar
Famous for the gorge, Cheddar village itself has much to offer. At the **Real Cheddar Cheese Dairy and Craft Village**, visitors can sample cheddar cheese and try their hand at a potters wheel or watch candle and lace making demonstrations. Restaurant. Open March to October, daily 1000–1600. Charge. Telephone (01934) 742810. **Cheddar Gorge** can be easily expored on foot or by climbing Jacob's Ladder (charge), a series of 274 steps leading to a look-out tower at the top of the cliffs. The area is littered with caves and tunnels which visitors can tour courtesy of **Cheddar Caves and Gorge**. Open May to September, daily 1000–1700; October to April, daily 1030–1630. Charge. Telephone (01934) 742343.

Ⓖ Chewton Cheese Dairy, Chewton Mendip
Tours are offered around this dairy which makes Cheddar cheese in the traditional manner. Also children's play area, animals and restaurant. Open daily 0900–1700. Charge for tours. Telephone (01761) 241666.

THE CTC

The CTC is Britain's largest national cycling organisation. Founded in 1878, the CTC has over 65,000 members and affiliates throughout the UK, and around 230 local groups. The CTC provides essential services for all leisure cyclists, whether riding on- or off-road, and works to promote cycling and protect cyclists' interests.

Free technical and touring advice

CTC membership makes day-to-day cycling easier. A resident expert cycling engineer answers technical queries about cycle buying, maintenance and equipment. And if you get ambitious about your cycling, the CTC's Touring Department has reams of information about cycling anywhere from Avon to Zimbabwe. Then, when it comes to getting kitted out, the CTC's mail order shop sells a wide variety of clothing and accessories in addition to books, maps and guidebooks, including other titles from HarperCollins Publishers.

CTC Helpdesk – telephone (01483) 417217

CTC members also receive *Cycle Touring and Campaigning* magazine free six times a year. *CT&C* takes pride in its journalistic independence. With reports on cycle trips all over the globe, forensic tests on bikes and equipment, and the most vigorous and effective pro-bike campaigning stance anywhere, *CT&C* is required reading for any cyclist.

CTC membership costs from £15 p.a.

It is not just members who benefit. The CTC works on behalf of all Britain's 22 million cycle owners. Its effective campaigning at national level helped to create the Government's National Cycling Strategy. It is lobbying for lower speed limits on country lanes; campaigning so that you can carry bikes on trains; working with Local Authorities to make towns more cycle-friendly, to ensure that roads are designed to meet cyclists' needs and kept well maintained; making sure that bridleways are kept open; and negotiating cyclists' access to canal towpaths.

Whatever kind of cyclist you are – mountain biker, Sunday potterer, bicycle commuter or out for the day with your family cycling is easier and safer with the CTC's knowledge and services in your saddlebag. The CTC is the essential accessory for every cyclist!

For further information contact:
CTC
69 Meadrow
Godalming
Surrey
GU7 3HS

Telephone (01483) 417217
Fax (01483) 426994
e-mail: cycling@ctc.org.uk
Website: http://www.ctc.org.uk